Genealogical

Periodical

Annual

INDEX

1962

Edited by

Ellen Stanley Rogers

Second Printing
by
HERITAGE BOOKS, INC.
3602 Maureen Ln., Bowie, MD 20715
1983

ISBN 0-917890-30-2

About the GPA INDEX . . .

The intent and aim of the GENEALOGICAL PERIODICAL ANNUAL INDEX is to provide genealogists, researchers and librarians with a comprehensive index to material published each year in all of the genealogical periodicals and to data of interest and value from other periodicals.

The GPA INDEX arrangement of this material is generally by surname or by location. Since many articles cannot be classified under either of these headings, the following topical headings have been added:

- Methods
- Sources
- Military Records
- Foreign Genealogy
- Emigrants
- Heraldry
- Nomenclature
- Poems & Songs
- Quizzes, cartoons, etc.
- Miscellaneous

Authors are also included in the INDEX, the term author designating the person who wrote, contributed, compiled or collected the material. A modified system of cross reference has been adapted to make the GPA INDEX especially helpful to researchers. Corrections appearing in a later issue are keyed to the original article. Where a title is not given or is not sufficiently explanatory, I have provided a title or added an informative note. In all cases, the primary objective has been to provide the researcher with a concise, convenient guide.

I appreciate the cooperation and encouragement from editors, societies and libraries who have stated a need for such an index to periodicals on their shelves. In this first year of publication, the GPA INDEX 1962 has attempted to fill this need.

Ellen Stanley Rogers

March 15, 1963

KEY TO GENEALOGICAL PERIODICALS

AFH - THE ARKANSAS FAMILY HISTORIAN, published by the Arkansas Genealogical Society, Box 237, Fayetteville, Ark. Editor: W. J. Lemke. Quarterly (Mar.): Vol. 1, 1962. Society membership, $2.00 per year. Single issues, $1.00 each. Pages per issue: 50. Size of page: 8½x11". No separate cover; stapled. Only issue available for inclusion in GPA INDEX 1962 is 1-3 (Sept.). Society news, p 2, 9, 47-50. List of researchers, p 25-7. Exchange, p 29-33. Queries, p 35-44.

AH - AMERICAN HERITAGE, The Magazine of History, published by American Heritage Publishing Co., Inc., 551 Fifth Ave., New York 17, N. Y. Editor: Bruce Catton. Bi-monthly (Dec.); Vol. 8 #2, Feb., 1962. Annual subscription, $15.00; single copies, $3.95. Pages per issue: 110-120. Size of page: 8½x11". Hard bound, profusely illus., color. Annual Index @ $1.00. Genealogical item included in GPA INDEX 1962, see Lewis.

ALA - THE ALABAMA GENEALOGICAL REGISTER, published by Willo Publishing Co., P. O. Box 284, Tuscaloosa, Ala. Editor: Elizabeth Wood Thomas. Quarterly (Mar.); Vol. 4, 1962. $5.00 per vol., $2.00 per issue. Pages per issue: 50. Yearly index, $2.50. Size of page: 8½x11". Heavy paper cover, bound. "Editor's Page" (notes on societies, research, etc.), 4-1, p 3; 4-2, p 51; 4-3, p 101; 4-4, p 151. Query section (Editor: Wilda Blewett McEllhiney), 4-1, p 45-9; 4-3, p 147-9.

AN - ANCESTRAL NOTES FROM CHEDWATO, published by Chedwato Service, Box 746, Burlington, Vt. Editors: Charles & Edna Townsend. Bi-monthly (Jan.); Vol. 9, 1962. $3.00 per vol., $.50 per issue. Pages per issue 24. Size of page: 5½x8½". No separate cover, stapled. Editor's Notes, 9-1, p 1; 9-2, p 25; 9-3, p 49; 9-5, p 97; 9-6, p 121. "Across Our Desks" (book notices), 9-1, p 15; 9-2, p 42-4; 9-3, p 65-9; 9-4, p 87-92; 9-5, p 117-20; 9-6, p 139-142. Queries in separate 4 to 6 page (8½x11") sheets, included with each issue. "Supplement from the Editor's Notebook" began in 1962, 12 pages each, included with each issue, and designated as SUP (numbered from 1 to 6) in the GPA INDEX 1962.

ANS - ANSEARCHIN' NEWS, published by the Memphis Genealogical Society. Editor: Mrs. Harry E. O'Hara, 5391 Shady Grove Terrace, Memphis, Tenn. Quarterly (Jan.); Vol. 9, 1962. $5.00 per year, $1.50 per issue. Pages per issue, about 42. Size of page, 8½x11". Punched for binder; binder cover for vol. sent in Jan. Full name index separate for each vol., included with Oct. issue, p 161-97 for 1962. Society news, 9-1, p 1; 9-2, p 40; 9-3, p 77; 9-4, p 120. "Over the Editor's Desk (book reviews & notices, publication news, notes, corrections): 9-1, p 2-5; 9-2, p 41-4, 46; 9-3, p 78; 9-4, p 121-5. Queries: 9-1, p 34-9; 9-2, p 70-76; 9-3, p 116-19; 9-4, p 157-60. Ads on back covers of issues.

AUS - AUSTIN GENEALOGICAL SOCIETY QUARTERLY, published by the Society. Editor: Mrs. Jean Halden Walker, 6301 Treadwell Blvd., Austin 3, Tex. Quarterly (Apr., May, Sept., Nov.); Vol. 3, 1962. $4.00 per year, $1.00 per issue (except April, which is $2.00). Pages in Vol. 3: 165. Size of page: 8½x11". No separate cover; punched for binder. Society news, general items: 3-1, p 1-4, 75-6; 3-2, p 77-8, 106-8; 3-3, p 109-15, 140; 3-4, p 142-5, 165. Queries:

3-4, p 164. Corrections to entries: 3-2, p 105; 3-3, p 139; 3-4, p 163. AGS Ancestor Listing: 3-1, p 5-75

BCT - BULLETIN OF THE CENTRAL TEXAS GENEALOGICAL SOCIETY, published by the Society. Editor: Mrs. R. G. Murrie, 3601 Gorman, Waco, Texas. Bi-monthly (Jan.-Feb.); Vol. 5, 1962. $3.00 per year, $.50 per issue. Pages per issue: about 12. Size of page: 8½x11". No separate cover, stapled at top. Supplement included with Vol. 5: Marriages of McLennan Co., Texas, p 39-56 (cont. from previous issue) and index to same, p 1-12 (to be completed in future issue). Society news, announcements, book notices: 5-1, p 1-5, 7-8; 5-2, p 1-2, 13; 5-3, p 1, 9-10; 5-4, p 1-2, 8-10; 5-5, p 1-2, 8-9; 5-6, p 1-3, 11-12. Queries: 5-1, p 6-7; 5-2, p 13-14; 5-3, p 2; 5-4, p 7-8; 5-5, p 7; 5-6, p 3-4, 10. Membership & Surname Directory: 5-2, p 3-12

CG - THE COLORADO GENEALOGIST, published by the Colorado Genealogical Society, 3386 West 34th Ave., Denver 11, Colo. Editor: Bernice Fitzsimmons Hathaway. Quarterly (Jan.); Vol. 23, 1962. $2.00 per vol., $.75 per issue. Pages per issue, about 30. Size of page; 8½x11". Paper cover, stapled. Society news, officers, accessions, general items: 23-1, p 1-2, 9-12, 25-8; 23-2, p 29-30; 46-8, 57-9; 23-3, p 61-2, 72, 74, 80, 85-8; 23-4, p 89-90, 95, 105-7, 114-8. Queries: 23-1, p 13; 23-2, p 44-7; 23-3, p 73-4; 23-4, p 96-8, 103-4. Corrections & additions (to Vol. 21, p 90 - Radford; and to Vol. 22, p 38 - Redding): 23-3, p 70-71

CSM - CHRONICLES OF ST. MARY'S, Monthly Bulletin of the St. Mary's County, Md., Historical Society. Editor: Edwin W. Beitzell, Abell, Md. Monthly; Vol. 10, 1962. $3.00 per year, single issues $1.00. Size of page: 8½x11". Pages per issue: 8. No separate cover; stapled. Articles pertaining to St. Mary's County, houses, shipping, Civil War, old families, index to county wills. Illustrations. Genealogical material only is included in GPA INDEX 1962.

DAL - LOCAL HISTORY & GENEALOGICAL SOCIETY, published by the Society, % Dallas Public Library, Dallas, Texas. Quarterly (Mar.); Vol. 8, 1962. $3.00 per vol., $.75 per issue. Size of page: 8½x11". Paper cover, stapled. 1962 issues contain "Index to Ancestors of Members of the Local Hist. & Gen. Society, Dallas, Tex.", in 4 parts, 170 pages.

DAR - DAUGHTERS OF THE AMERICAN REVOLUTION MAGAZINE, published by the National Society Daughters of the American Revolution, Administration Bldg., 1776 D St., N. W., Washington 6, D. C. Editor: Miss Mabel W. Winslow. Monthly (except July & Aug.); Vol. 96, 1962. Issue #6 is called June-July; issue #8 is called Aug.-Sept.; no #7 or #9. $2.00 per year, $.35 per issue. Size of page: 8½x11". "Genealogical Department" (also called "Genealogical Source Material"), edited by Beatrice Kenyon, later by Mrs. Ivan T. Johnson. This section only is included in the GPA INDEX 1962, with one exception: see Shannon. Index for 1962 issues ("Index for the Genealogical Dept. of the DAR Magazine"), prepared by John Frederick Dorman, 2311 Connecticut Ave., Washington 8, D. C., is available at $2.00. Queries: 96-1, p 38, 120; 96-2, p 163, 212; 96-3, p 336; 96-4, p 389, 461; 96-5, p 507, 518; 96-6, p 549; 96-8, p 619, 628; 96-11, p 711, 718; 96-12, p 745. Corrections (to query in 96-8, p 619): in 96-10, p 661. Library accessions: issues # 4, 6 and 12.

DS - THE DETROIT SOCIETY FOR GENEALOGICAL RESEARCH MAGAZINE, published by the Society, % Burton Historical Collection, Detroit Public Library, Detroit 2,

Mich. Editor: Miss Lucy Mary Kellogg. Quarterly (Fall); Vol. 25 #3, Spring 1962: #4, Summer; Vol. 26 #1, Fall, 1962: #2, Winter. $3.00 per vol., $1.00 per issue ($.75 to members). Pages per issue: 48. Size of page: 8½x11". Heavy paper cover; saddle stitched. Subject Index of 1 page published in last issue of each vol. News and notes, meeting reports, etc.: 25-3, p 134-5, 138; 25-4, p 178-9, 183; 26-1, p 19, 21, 40, 42-3, 46; 26-2, p 87-8, 92. Queries: 25-3, p 136-7; 25-4, p 180-2; 26-1, p 44-5; 26-2, p 89-91. Corrections & additions: see Cooley; Sutton; Sutphin; Lockwood; Baker, in GPA INDEX 1962.

ECH - ECHOES (FROM THE EAST TENNESSEE HISTORICAL SOCIETY), published by the Society, Lawson McGhee Library, 217 Market St., Knoxville 2, Tenn. Editor: Dr. S. J. Folmsbee. Associate Editor: Pollyanna Creekmore. Three issues in 1962 (Mar., Oct., Dec.), together with the annual "Publications", with membership, $5.00. Customarily a quarterly. Single issues vary at $.50 to $1.00 each. Vol. 8, 1962. Photostats (Verifax) @ $.25 per page. Pages per issue: 8 to 18. Size of page: 8½x11". No separate cover; stapled. Society notes, accessions, book notes, general items: 8-1, p 233-43, 247; 8-2, p 251-8; 8-4, p 266-70; Queries: 8-1, p 248-50; 8-2, p 262-5; 8-4, p 271-3. Item of genealogical interest from PUBLICATIONS, #34, 1962: See Tenn., Washington Co. Taxpayers, 1778.

EIH - ESSEX INSTITUTE HISTORICAL COLLECTIONS, published by The Essex Institute, Salem, Mass. Managing Editor: Dean A. Fales, Jr. Quarterly (Jan.); Vol. 98, 1962. $5.00 per year. Items included in GPA INDEX: see Ingalls; Mass., Beverly.

FC - THE FILSON CLUB HISTORY QUARTERLY, published by The Filson Club, 118 West Breckenridge St., Louisville 3, Ky. Quarterly (Jan.); Vol. 36, 1962. $6.00 per year, $1.50 per issue. Full name index bound in issue #4, 32 pages. Queries: 36-1, p 63; 36-2, p 195; 36-3, p 293. Only articles of genealogical interest are included in the GPA INDEX 1962

FF - FAULKNER FACTS & FIDDLINGS, published by the Faulkner County (Ark.) Historical Society, Conway, Ark. Editor: Guy W. Murphy. Quarterly (Mar.); Vol. 4, 1962. Genealogical items from issue #1 (Mar.) only are included in GPA INDEX 1962.

FGQ - FLINT GENEALOGICAL QUARTERLY, published by the Flint Genealogical Society, % Mrs. Eldon P. Gundry, 1909 Ramsey Blvd., Flint 3, Mich. Editor: Mrs. Walter Mayer. Quarterly (Jan.); Vol. 4, 1962. $2.00 per year, $.30 per issue. Pages per issue, 20. Size of page: 5½x8½". Photostats @ $.40 per page. Heavy cover; saddle stitched. Surname index mailed with Oct. issue as supplement. Society news, membership list, general items: 4-1, p 1, 9; 4-2, p 21, 39; 4-3, p 41, 46-7, 59-60; 4-4, p 61, 80. Queries: 4-1, p 18; 4-2, p 32; 4-3, p 48. Corrections (to 3-3, p 43-4; to 3-4, p 54, 58, 61, 63, 65): in 4-1, p 20.

G&H - GENEALOGY & HISTORY, published & edited by Adrian Ely Mount, Box 1717, Washington 13, D. C. Quarterly (Mar.); Vol. 23, 1962. $2.00 per year. Pages per issue: 32. Size of page: 5½x8½". Currently consists of Index to issues #18-114, with approximately 14 pages per issue of books, etc., for sale, and 1 page of classified ads, occasional queries.

GH - THE GENEALOGICAL HELPER, published by The Everton Publishers, 526 North Main St., Logan, Utah. Quarterly (Mar.); Vol. 16, 1962. $3.00 per year. Pages per issue: 32, except 160 in Sept. Size of page: 8½x11". No separate cover; saddle stitched (Sept. issue is bound); punched for binder. Book notices, announcements. ads, general items throughout each issue. Index to Vol. 16 is in 16-4, p 260-71. Sept. issue (16-3) contains "1962 Directory of Genealogists", p 71-213. Queries: 16-1, p 11-15; 16-2, p 48-64; 16-4, p 233-48.

GM - GEORGIA MAGAZINE, published & edited by Ann E. Lewis, P. O. Box 4047, Decatur, Ga. Bi-monthly; Dec.-Jan. 1962 is Vol. 5, #4; June-July is Vol. 6, #1. $3.00 per year; $.50 per single issue. Pages per issue: 35 to 60. Size of page: 8½x11". Heavy paper cover, saddle stitched. Illustrations, photos. Articles pertain to Georgia history, etc. Each issue contains "What's Your Family Line?", edited by Adelle Bartlett Harper. This feature also contains queries.

GN - GENEALOGICAL NEWSLETTER & RESEARCH AIDS, published & edited by Inez Waldenmaier, 854 Warner Bldg., Washington 4, D. C. Quarterly (Spring): Vol. 8, 1962. $5.00 per year. Pages per issue: about 45. Size of page: 8½x11". Heavy paper cover; stapled; punched for binder. Contains "Index to Miscellaneous Bible Records," "Newly Published County Histories," "Newly Published Family Histories." News items, new books, etc.: 8-1, p 1-8, 32; 8-2, p 41-4, 54, 83; 8-3, p 91-4, 101, 132; 8-4, p 133-6, 172, 177-8. Queries: 8-1, p 33-40; 8-2, p 84-90; 8-3, p 127-32; 8-4, p 173-7.

HG - THE HOOSIER GENEALOGIST, published by the Indiana Historical Society, 140 N. Senate Ave., Indianapolis, Ind. Editor: Miss Nell W. Reeser. Bi-monthly (Jan.-Feb.); Vol. 2, 1962. $5.00 membership includes HG. Single issues available only to members of the Indiana Historical Society @ $.25 each. Pages per issue, 10 to 12. Size of page: 8½x11". Photocopies (Xerox) @ $.25 per page. No separate cover; stapled. Index for 1962 issues included with Vol. 2 #6 as p 11-12. Notes, accessions of the Indiana State Library: 2-1, p 5-6, 10; 2-2, p 1, 4, 7-10; 2-3, p 1, 7-10; 2-4, p 1, 8-10, 12; 2-5, p 1-2, 4-5, 11-14; 2-6, p 1, 9, 12. Queries: 2-1, p 7-8; 2-2, p 8; 2-3, p 9; 2-4, p 11-12; 2-5, p 9-11; 2-6, p 10.

HO - HOBBIES: The Magazine for Collectors, published by Lightner Publishing Corp., 1006 S. Michigan Ave., Chicago 5, Ill. Monthly (Mar.); Vol. 66 #11, Jan., 1962; Vol. 67 #1, Mar. 1962. #3.50 per year; $.50 per issue. Each issue contains "At the Sign of the Family Crest," conducted by Hazel Kraft Eilers; article on a specific family name with coat of arms and data on immigrants, etc. Query section in each issue.

HOU - THE GENEALOGICAL RECORD, published by the Houston Genealogical Forum, % Houston Public Library, Houston 2, Tex. Editor: James R. Mitchell. Quarterly (Mar.): Vol. 4, 1962. $2.00 per vol., $.75 per issue. Pages per issue: 12. Size of page: 8½x11". No separate cover; stapled. Only issue published in 1962 was #1, March. Society news, accessions: 4-1, p 1, 12. Queries: 4-1, p 11. Photocopies @ $.35 per page.

HPO - HISTORICAL & PHILOSOPHICAL SOCIETY OF OHIO BULLETIN, published by the Society, Room 205 Library, Univ. of Cincinnati, Cincinnati 21, Ohio. Quarterly (Jan.); Vol. 20, 1962. $10.00 per year. "Genealogical Department" in each issue is edited by Marie Dickore.

HT - HARTFORD TIMES, published by Kenneth K. Burke, edited by Robert W. Lucas,

Hartford, Conn. $4.00 per year (Monday issue only); $2.00 for 6 mo.; $1.00 for 3 mo. Monday Special edition contains feature "Genealogical Questions & Answers," edited by Louise Benn MacNeely. Mainly an exchange medium, rarely notes or source material.

IDA - IDAHO GENEALOGICAL SOCIETY QUARTERLY, published by the Society, 610 Julia Davis Drive, Boise, Idaho. Editor: Dale F. Walden. Quarterly (Mar.); Vol. 5, 1962. $2.00 per vol., $.50 per issue. Pages per issue: about 24. Size of page: 8½x11". Heavy paper cover, stapled. Society news, officers, accessions, general items: 5-1, p 1-9, 15-17; 5-2, p 1-8, 13-14, 16; 5-3, p 1-8, 17a-18; 5-4, p 1-5, 8, 11, 18, 22, 24. Queries: 5-1, p 22-4 (see correction to p 24 in 5-2, p 21); 5-2, p 21-2; 5-3, p 23-4; 5-4, p 23-4.

JC - MAGAZINE OF THE JEFFERSON COUNTY HISTORICAL SOCIETY, published by the Society, % Mr. Frank W. Buckles, Gap View Farm, Charles Town, W. Va. Editor: A. D. Kenamond. Yearly (Dec.?); Vol. 28, Dec. 1962. $1.35 per copy. Membership in Society @ $1.00 includes magazine. Pages per issue: 60. Size of page: 6x9". Heavy paper cover, saddle stitched. Society notes, officers, members: p 3-12.

JNC - JOURNAL OF NORTH CAROLINA GENEALOGY (Formerly THE NORTH CAROLINIAN), published & edited by William Perry Johnson, P. O. Box 531, Raleigh, N. C. Quarterly (Mar.); Vol. 8, 1962. $7.00 per year (4 issues plus index); $1.50 per issue. 1962 issues for $6.00; Surname Index of 18 pages, @ $1.00. Pages per issue: 40. Size of page: 8½x11". Paper cover, saddle stitched. Editor's Page: 8-1, p 918; 8-2, p 958; 8-3, p 998; 8-4, p 1038. Accessions (by N. C. State Dept. of Archives & History, and by State Library): 8-1, p 944-6; 8-2, p 984-7; 8-3, p 1022-4; 8-4, p 1070-72. Ads: 8-1, p 918, 947-50, 955-6; 8-2, p 988-91, 996; 8-3, p 998, 1024, 1034-6; 8-4, p 1072-6. Queries: 8-1, p 951-4; 8-2, p 992-6; 8-3, p 1035-6.

JSH - THE JOURNAL OF SOUTHERN HISTORY, published by the Southern Historical Association, 1407 Sherwood Ave., Richmond, Va. Managing Editor: William W. Abbot. Quarterly (Feb.): Vol. 28, 1962. $5.00 per year; $1.25 per issue.

KCG - THE KANSAS CITY GENEALOGIST, published by the Heart of America Genealogical Society, 146 N. Lawn, Kansas City 23, Mo. Editor: Mrs. Darlene R. Appell. Monthly until July 1962; quarterly thereafter(July); Vol. 2, # 11, Jan. 1962; Vol. 3 # 1, July 1962. $2.00 per year, single issues (Jan.-June) $.25 and (July & Oct.) $.50. Pages per issue: up to 12 prior to July; up to 18 thereafter. Size of page: 8½x11". No separate cover; stapled. Society news, book notices: 2-11, p 1; 2-12, p 1-2; 2-13, p 1-2; 2-14, p 1; 2-15, p 1-2; 2-16, p 1, 4; 3-1, p 1, 3; 3-2, p 1. Queries: 2-13, p 8; 2-14, p 8; 2-15, p 8; 2-16, p 6, 8; 3-1, p 2, 16; 3-2, p 2, 18. Membership Roster (10 pages) included as supplement.

KG - THE KENTUCKY GENEALOGIST, published & edited by Miss Martha Porter Miller, P. O. Box 4894, Washington 8, D. C. Quarterly (Jan.): Vol. 4, 1962. $5.00 per vol., $1.50 per issue. Pages per issue: 40. Size of page: 6x9". Heavy paper cover, saddle stitched. Full name index (of 41 pages) bound in Oct. issue. "Odds & Ends" (notes): 4-3, p 82; 4-4, p 122. Queries: 4-1, p 38-40; 4-2, p 78-80; 4-3, p 117-120; 4-4, p 158-60. Corrections (to 4-2, p 57): 4-4, p 131.

LA - GENEALOGICAL REGISTER, published by the Louisiana Genealogical & Historical Society, Box 335, Baton Rouge, La. Editor: Mary Elizabeth Sanders. Quarterly

(Mar.); Vol. 9, 1962. Membership @ $3.00 per year includes magazine. No single issues; sold only by Volume. Vol. 9 (1962) @ $4.00. Indexes for 2-year periods available @ $1.00 per Index. Society news, accessions, book notices: 9-1, p 1-2, 13; 9-2, p 19, 26-7; 9-3, p 40-1, 48; 9-4, p 49, 54, 61. Queries: 9-1, p 14-16; 9-2, p 30-2; 9-3, p 46-8; 9-4, p 62-4.

LIH - THE JOURNAL OF LONG ISLAND HISTORY, published by the Long Island Historical Society, 128 Pierrepont St., Brooklyn 1, N. Y. Bi-annual: Vol. 2, 1962. Single issues $1.00 each. Pages per issue 56 to 66. Size of page: 6x9". Heavy paper cover; saddle stitched.

LM - LAUREL MESSENGER, published by the Historical & Genealogical Society of Somerset Co., Pa., P. O. Box 533, Somerset, Pa. Editors: Eber Cockley & Robert G. Sanner. Quarterly (Feb.); Vol. 3, 1962. Single issues for 1962 not available

MDG - THE MARYLAND & DELAWARE GENEALOGIST, published & edited by Raymond B. Clark, Jr., P. O. Box 9394, Mid City Sta., Washington 5, D. C. Quarterly in future (Jan.); Vol. 3 #2, Winter 1961-2; #3, Spring; #4, Summer; no Fall issue for 1962. $5.00 per vol., $1.50 per issue. Pages per issue: about 25. Size of page: 8½x11". Heavy paper cover; stapled. Surname index in final issue of vol.; in 1962, in 3-4, pages 87-91. Notes, general items: 3-2, p 27, 47, 50; 3-3, p 52-61, 64; 3-4, p 73 & back cover. Queries: 3-2, p 49-50; 3-3, p 71; 3-4, p 86. Corrections (to Vol. 3, p 18, 28, 49, 52): 3-4, p 93.

MGS - BULLETIN OF THE MARYLAND GENEALOGICAL SOCIETY, published by the Society, 212 Holland Rd., Severna Park, Md. Editor: Mrs. C. C. Meyer III. Quarterly (Jan.); Vol. 3, 1962. $2.00 per vol., $.25 per issue ($.40 for Oct. exchange issue). Pages per issue: up to 16. Size of page: 8½x11". No separate cover; stapled. Society news, book notes: 3-1, p 1-4, 12; 3-2, p 13-17, 22; 3-3, p 23-5, 29-30; 3-4, p 34-42, 45-6. Membership & Exchange List (9 pages) in Oct. issue. Queries: 3-1, p 6; 3-2, p 17, 22; 3-3, p 25-6 and 29-30; 3-4, p 43-4.

MGX - MISSISSIPPI GENEALOGICAL EXCHANGE, edited & published by Mrs. Katie-Prince W. Esker, 314 Louisville St., Starkville, Miss. Quarterly (Mar.); Vol. 8, 1962. $4.00 per vol.; not sold by single issue. Size of page: 8½x11". Issues included in GPA INDEX 1962 are #1 & 2 (combined issue), March & June, 1962. Queries: 8-1&2, p 34-40.

MH - MICHIGAN HERITAGE, published by the Kalamazoo Valley Genealogical Society, Kalamazoo Public Museum, 315 S. Rose St., Kalamazoo, Mich. Editor: Dr. Ethel W. Williams. Quarterly (Autumn): Vol. 3 #3, Spring 1962; Vol. 4 #1, Autumn 1962. Membership @ $3.00 per year includes magazine; single issues $1.50 to members, $2.00 to non-members. Pages per issue: about 70. Size of page: 8½x11". Heavy paper cover; stapled. Society news, book notes, general items, ads, etc.: 3-3, p 140, 143, 177-80; 3-4, p 237-240; 4-1, p 68-70. Queries: 4-1, p 67. Vol. 4 #2 not released in time for inclusion in GPA INDEX 1962.

MHM - MARYLAND HISTORICAL MAGAZINE, published by the Maryland Historical Society, 201 W. Monument St., Baltimore 1, Md. Editor: Richard Walsh. Quarterly (Mar.): Vol. 57, 1962. $4.00 per year; $1.00 per issue. Pages per issue: about 74. Size of page: 6x9". Genealogical items only included in GPA INDEX 1962. Queries: 57-1, p 71-2; 57-2, p 173-5; 57-3, p 282-3; 57-4, p 394-6.

MHR - MISSOURI HISTORICAL REVIEW, published by the State Historical Society of Missouri, Columbia, Mo. Editor: Richard S. Brownlee, 119 S. Elson St., Kirksville, Mo. Quarterly (Oct.): Vol. 56 #2, Jan. 1962; Vol. 57 #1, Oct. 1962. $1.00 per year. Material of genealogical interest only is included in the GPA INDEX 1962.

MHT - THE MT. HOOD TRACKERS, published by the Mt. Hood Genealogical Forum, P. O. Box 426, Estacada, Ore. Acting Editor: Mrs. Harlan Olsen. Three issues per year (Mar., June, Oct.); Vol. 4, 1962. $2.50 per year; $.75 per issue. Pages per issue: up to 20. Size of page: 8½x11". Paper cover; stapled. Society news, book notices: 4-1, p 1-2, 14; 4-2, p 1-5; 4-3, p 1-2. Queries: 4-1, p 3-5; 4-2, p 3, 5; 4-3, p 3-5. Query index: 4-2, p 2, 6-12.

MI - MICHIGANA, published by the Western Michigan Genealogical Society, 70 Bostwick St., Grand Rapids, Mich. Editor: Mildred L. Adams. Quarterly (Feb.): Vol. 8, 1962. $2.50 per year; $.75 per issue. Pages per issue: 6 to 8. Size of page: 8½x11". Photocopies @ $.25 per page. No separate cover; stapled. Society news: 8-1, p 1-2, 4-6; 8-2, p 1-2, 4, 6; 8-3, p 1-2, 4-6; 8-4, p 1-3, 5, 8. Queries: 8-1, p 1-2; 8-2, p 1; 8-3, p 1-2, 4; 8-4, p 2-4.

ML - MISSING LINKS, published by Chedwato Service, P. O. Box 746, Burlington, Vt. Editor: Edna W. Townsend. Monthly (Aug.): Vol. 1 #1-5 (Aug.-Dec., 1962). $3.00 per vol., $.35 per issue. Pages per issue: 20. Size of page: 5½x8½". No separate cover; stapled. Contains family records, census records, etc.

NB - THE NEW BERN MIRROR, published & edited by J. Gaskill McDaniel, 510 Pollock St., New Bern, N. C. Weekly (Fri.) newspaper: $2.50 per year, $1.25 for 6 mo. & contains weekly column, "Historical Gleanings," edited by Elizabeth Moore, dealing with Craven County, N. C. history & genealogy.

NCR - THE NORTH CAROLINA HISTORICAL REVIEW, published by the State Dept. of Archives & History, Raleigh, N. C. Editor: Christopher Crittenden. Quarterly (Winter): Vol. 39 #1, Winter (or Jan.) 1962. $3.00 per year; $.75 per issue. Material of genealogical interest only is included in GPA INDEX 1962.

NE - THE NEW ENGLAND HISTORICAL & GENEALOGICAL REGISTER, published by the New England Historic Genealogical Society, 9 Ashburton Place, Boston 8, Mass. Editor: Gilbert Harry Doane. Quarterly (Jan.): Vol. 116, 1962. $7.50 per vol., $2.00 per issue. Pages per issue: 80. Size of page: 6x9". Heavy paper cover; stitched. Full name index in each vol. bound in following Jan. issue. Proceedings, accessions, society notes: Jan., p 71-6, 81-3; Apr., p 143-50, 154-6; July, 226-30, 232-5; Oct., 306-8, 311-15. Queries: Jan., p 83-4; Apr., p 156-157; July, p 235-6; Oct., p 315-7. Corrections (to Vol. 115, 1961): Jan. p 383.

NGS - NATIONAL GENEALOGICAL SOCIETY QUARTERLY, published by the Society, 1921 Sunderland Place, N. W., Washington 6, D. C. Editor: Milton Rubincam, succeeded by John Insley Coddington. Quarterly (Mar.): Vol. 50, 1962. $6.00 per year ($5.00 to members); $1.50 per issue ($1.25 to members). Pages per issue: about 64. Size of page: 7x10". Heavy paper cover, saddle stitched. Full name index (about 16 pages) mailed with following March issue. Each issue contains 16 page bound-in supplement "Index to Revolutionary War Pensions." Oct. issue (#4) not released in time for inclusion in GPA INDEX 1962. Society news, membership lists, notes, ads: 50-1, p 1-2, 18, 36, 48-65; 50-2, p 67-8, 94, 113, 119-20, 124-6, 128-30; 50-3, p 131-2, 168-73.

NJ - THE GENEALOGICAL MAGAZINE OF NEW JERSEY, published by the Genealogical Society of N. J., % Mrs. Dorothy A. Stratford, 132 W. Franklin St., Bound Brook, N. J. Editor: Donald A. Sinclair. Three issues per year (Jan., May, Sept.): Vol. 37, 1962. $5.00 per vol., single issues $2.00 (discount to members). Pages per issue: 48. Size of page: 6x9". Heavy paper cover, saddle stitched. Index issued in Feb. following. Work in Progress (and not in progress): 37-1, p 35; 37-2, p 96; 37-3, p 110. Corrections (to 36:141, 37:87, 90, 91; 33:70): 37-3.

NJG - THE NEW JERSEY GENESIS, published & edited by Harold A. Sonn, 105-C Troy Drive, Springfield, N. J. Quarterly (Oct.); Vol. 9 #2, Jan. 1962. $3.00 per year, $1.00 per issue. Pages per issue: 12. Size of page: 8½x11". No separate cover. Topic Index (3 pages) to Vols. 8 & 9: 9-4, p 386-8. "N. J. Family Index," published (irregular) by NJG. Notes, book notices, items of interest: 9-2, p 353-8, p 361-4; 9-3, p 366, 370-6; 9-4, p 378-9, 382-4, 388; 10-1, p 389-90, 394-5, 397-400. Queries: 9-2, p 353-5; 9-3, p 368-70, 374; 9-4, p 380-82; 10-1, p 392-4, 400. Additions & corrections (to Oct. 1961 NJG - Probasco family), 9-2, p 355: (to July 1961 NJG - Stey(n)mets family), 9-2, p 364: (to April 1962 NJG, p 371 - Ford family), 9-4, p 384.

NM - NEW MEXICO GENEALOGIST, published by the New Mexico Genealogical Society, P. O. Box 8734, Albuquerque, N. Mex. Editor: Dr. Albert R. Elwell. Quarterly (Jan.); Vol. 1 # 1, Oct. 1962 (sole issue published in 1962). $2.00 per year, $.50 per issue, photostats @ $.35 per page. Pages per issue: 16. Size of page: 8½x11". No separate cover; stapled. Society news, membership list, etc.: 1-1, p 1-2, 11-13. Queries: 1-1, p 16.

NYR - THE NEW YORK GENEALOGICAL AND BIOGRAPHICAL RECORD, published by the New York Gen. & Biog. Society, 122 East 58th St., New York 22, N. Y. Quarterly (Jan.): Vol. 93, 1962. $6.00 per year, $2.00 per issue, photocopies @ $.50 per page. Pages per issue: 64. Size of page: 6x9¼. Heavy paper cover, saddle stitched. Society news, accessions, ads, etc.: 93-1, p 55-6, 61-4; 93-2, p 115-17, 125-8; 93-3, p 177-80, 182-4, 189-92; 93-4, p 249-50, 253-6, and on back covers. Additions & corrections (to Vol. 61, p 34 - Harned, Piety) (to Vol. 71, p 275 - Van Kouwenhoven-Conover, Rapelje, Lott) (to Vol. 89, p 240 - Dibble) (to Vol. 90, p 240 - Arnett, Kollock) (to Vol. 91, p 1-4 - LeGrand) (to Vol. 91, p 55) (to Vol. 91, p 77 - Staats, Quick) (to Vol. 91, p 93 - Polhemus, Van Barkelo) (to Vol. 91, p 152) (to Vol. 91, p 158 - Yale) (to Vol. 91, p 219 - Stryker): see 93-4, p 243-7.

OGS - REPORT, published by the Ohio Genealogical Society, 454 Park Ave., West, Mansfield, Ohio. Editor: Mrs. Betsy Geib. Bi-monthly (Mar.): Vol. 2, 1962. $5.00 per year, $1.00 per issue to members ($1.50 to non-members). Pages per issue: 4. Size of page: 16x22" (in newspaper format). Contains Ohio history, society news, book announcements, etc. Queries: 2-1, p 4; 2-2, p 4; 2-3, p 4; 2-5, p 4.

OH - OUR HERITAGE, published by The San Antonio Genealogical & Historical Society, P. O. Box 6383, Alamo Heights Sta., San Antonio 9, Texas. Editor: Mrs. James H. Clark. Quarterly (Oct.): Vol. 3 #2, Jan. 1962. $5.00 per vol., $1.25 per issue. Pages per issue: about 30. Size of page: 8½x11". Heavy paper cover; bound. Society news, book reviews, accessions, etc.: 3-2, p 31, 56-60; 3-3, p 61, 85-92; 3-4, p 93, 112-20; 4-1, p 1, 22-7. Queries: 3-2, p 54-6; 3-3, p 80-84; 3-4, p 110-11; 4-1, p 20-22.

OKL - OKLAHOMA GENEALOGICAL SOCIETY QUARTERLY, published by the Society, P.O. Box 7652, Oklahoma City, Okla. Editor: Mrs. Dorothy DeWitt Wilkinson. Quarterly (Mar.): Vol. 7, 1962. $4.00 per year ($3.00 with membership), $.25 and $1.00 per issue. Pages per issue: 22. Size of page: 8½x11". Can provide photostats. No separate cover; stapled. Society news, general items, accessions: 7-1, p 275-6, 289-90; 7-2, p 291-3, 297, 307-12; 7-3, p 313-6, 323-7, 332-3; 7-4, p 1. Queries: 7-1, p 285-8; 7-2, p 303-7; 7-3, p 328-32; 7-4, p 12-22. Surname-query Index (Directory issue): 7-1, p 277-84; 7-4, p 1-11.

OR - OHIO RECORDS AND PIONEER FAMILIES, published & edited by Esther W. Powell, 36 N. Highland Ave., Akron 3, Ohio. Quarterly (Jan.): Vol. 3, 1962. $5.00 per vol., $1.50 per issue. Pages per issue: 50. Size of page: 8½x11". Heavy paper cover, bound. Surname index (22 pages) bound in #4. "Editor's Notes," etc.: 3-1, p 1-2; 3-2, p 51; 3-3, p 103-4; 3-4, p 153. Queries: 3-1, p 45-50 (correction to Query #264 appears in 3-3, p 103); 3-2, p 97-102; 3-3, p 148-152; 3-4, p 196-200. Corrections (to 2-4): 3-1, p 2; (to Vols. 2 & 3): 3-3, p 103.

PGM - THE PENNSYLVANIA GENEALOGICAL MAGAZINE, published by the Genealogical Society of Penn., 1300 Locust St., Philadelphia 7, Pa. Bi-annual (Spring & Fall; 4 issues make one vol.): Vol. 22 #3 & 4, 1962. $3.00 for Fall issue, $1.50 for Spring issue. Pages in Spring issue: 30. In Fall issue: 124. Size of page: 7x10". No separate cover on Spring issue; stapled. Heavy paper cover on Fall issue; bound. Photocopies @ $1.00 per page. Full name index, 22-4, p 284-313. Society news, book notices, etc.: 22-4, p 276-8, 282.

POR - MONTHLY BULLETIN OF THE GENEALOGICAL FORUM OF PORTLAND, ORE., published by the Forum, 4540 N. E. 22nd Ave., Portland 11, Ore. Editor: Mrs. Clarence W. Carey. Monthly (except July-Aug.): Vol. 11 # 5, Jan. 1962. Vol. 12 # 1, Sept. 1962. $3.00 per year; $.25 per issue. Pages per issue: 8. Size of page: 8½x11". No separate cover; stapled. Supplement, titled "Jackson Co., Ore. 1860 Census," pages 57-60 (includes Walker, J. H., to Zimmerman); and "Jackson Co., Ore. 1870 Census," pages 1-36 (Ackley to Lewis, Ruthabel), included with 1962 issues. Society news, book notices, ads, general notes: 11-5, p 33-4, 38, 40; 11-6, p 41-2, 48; 11-7, p 49-50, 54, 56; 11-8, p 57-8, 61-4; 11-9, p 65-66, 68, 72; 11-10, p 73-4, 76-80; 12-1, p 1-2, 4, 6, 8; 12-2, p 9-10, 12, 14, 16; 12-3, p 17-18, 21, 24; 12-4, p 25-6, 30, 32. Queries: 11-5, p 36-7; 11-6, p 44-5; 11-7, p 51; 11-8, p 59; 11-9, p 67; 11-10, p 75; 12-1, p 3; 12-2, p 11; 12-3, p 19; 12-4, p 27.

RIH - RHODE ISLAND HISTORY, published by the Rhode Island Historical Society, 52 Power Ave., Providence 6, R. I. Quarterly (Jan.): Vol. 21, 1962. Rarely publishes genealogy; however, currently contains genealogical material; see Smith entry, GPA INDEX 1962.

REF - THE REFLECTOR, published by the Amarillo Genealogical Society, % Mary E. Bivins Memorial Library, P. O. Box 2171, Amarillo, Texas. Editor: LeRoy Hutton. Quarterly (Jan.): Vol. 4, 1962. Pages per issue: about 12. Size of page: 8½x11". No separate cover; stapled at top. Membership Roster & Ancestral Index: 4-4, p 40-50. Society news, book notices, etc.: 4-1, p 1-3; 4-2, p 12-14; 4-3, p 24-6; 4-4, p 38-9. Queries: 4-1, p 4; 4-2, p 15.

RK - THE REGISTER OF THE KENTUCKY HISTORICAL SOCIETY, published by the Society, Old State House, Frankfort, Ky. Editor: G. Glenn Clift. Quarterly (Jan.):

Vol. 60, 1962. $5.00 per vol., $2.00 per issue, photostats @ $.75 per page. Pages per issue: 84. Size of page: 6x9". Heavy paper cover; bound. Material of genealogical interest only is included in GPA INDEX 1962. Queries: 60-2, p 153-5.

SAR - SONS OF THE AMERICAN REVOLUTION MAGAZINE, published by the Sons of the American Revolution, 2412 Massachusetts Ave., N. W., Washington, D. C. Quarterly (July): Vol. 56 #3, Jan. 1962; Vol. 57 #1, July 1962. $2.00 per year, $.50 per issue. Primarily society news, general articles of history, etc. Accessions of the Library: 57-2, p 20-23. Queries: 56-3, p 24; 56-4, p 33; 57-1, p 26; 57-2, p 19.

SCH - SOUTH CAROLINA HISTORICAL MAGAZINE, published by the S. C. Historical Society, Fireproof Building, Charleston, S. C. Editor: Mrs. Granville T. Prior. Quarterly (Jan.); Vol. 63, 1962. $6.00 per year, $2.00 per issue ($1.75 to members), photocopies @ $.60 per page. Pages per issue: 64. Size of page: 6x9". Heavy paper cover, bound. Full name index: 63-4, p 247-68. Accessions, publications, society news, etc.: 63-1, p 59-60; 63-2, p 119-24; 63-3, p 188-93; 63-4, p 242-5. Queries: 63-1, p 59-60; 63-2, p 121; 63-3, p 192-193; 63-4, p 244-5, and back cover.

SEA - BULLETIN OF THE SEATTLE GENEALOGICAL SOCIETY, published by the Society, 4707 Greenwood Ave. North, Seattle 3, Wash. Editor: Arthur D. Fiske. Monthly (except July-Aug.): Vol. 11 #5, Jan. 1962: Vol. 12 #1, Sept. 1962. $3.00 per year. Pages per issue: 8 to 12. Size of page: 8½x11". No separate cover; stapled. Supplements included with 1962 issues: "Asotin Co., Washington Territory 1885 Auditor's Census," p 11-36; "Chehalis Co., Washington, 1871 Census," p 1-4. Society news, accessions: 11-5, p 133-4, 137-8; 11-6, p 139-40, 145-6; 11-7, p 147-8, 153, 156; 11-8, p 157-8, 163; 11-9, p 167-8, 174-6; 11-10, p 177-8; 12-1, p 189-90, 192, 196; 12-2, p 199, 206, 208; 12-3, p 209, 215-16; 12-4, p 217-18, 222. Queries: 11-5, p 137; 11-6, p 145; 11-7, p 155-6; 11-8, p 166; 11-9, p 174-5; 11-10, p 179-88 (includes Index to Queries in Vols. 1-5 of Bulletin); 12-1, p 197-8; 12-2, p 201-4 (includes Index to Queries in Vols. 6-9 of Bulletin, from "A" to Hyland), 207; 12-3, p 211-14 (conclusion of Index to Queries, Vols. 6-9); 12-4, p 225-6.

SGX - THE SOUTHERN GENEALOGIST'S EXCHANGE QUARTERLY, published & edited by Mrs. Aurora C. Shaw, 2525 Oak St., Jacksonville 4, Fla. Quarterly (Spring): Vol. 3 (series II); No. 21, Spring 1962. (#22, Summer; #23 Fall; #24, Winter). $5.00 per year, $1.50 per issue. Pages per issue: 46 to 52. Size of page: 8½x11". Paper cover; stapled. Finding List to 1962 material: 3-24, p 47-50. Surname Index to queries in 1962: 3-24, p 45-6. News items, book notices, ads: 3-21, p 1-6, 10, 14, 30; 3-22, p 1-3, 28, 52; 3-23, p 1-2, 12, 17, 34, 38; 42; 3-24, p 1-6, 18, 30, 42, 50. Queries: 3-21, p 43-50; 3-22, p 49-51; 3-23, p 39-42; 3-24, p 43-4.

STA - BULLETIN OF THE STAMFORD GENEALOGICAL SOCIETY, published by the Society, 96 Broad St., Stamford, Conn. Editor: Robert W. Carder. Monthly (except June, July & Aug.): Vol. 4 #5, Jan. 1962; Vol. 5 # 1, Sept. 1962. $2.00 per year, $.25 per issue, Verifax copies @ $.05 per page. Pages per issue: 10 to 12. Size of page: 8½x11". No separate cover. Directory of Ancestral Names: 5-1, p 7-27. Society notes, book notices, accessions, etc.: 4-5, p 55-6; 4-6, p 65-8, 74; 4-7, p 75-7, 86; 4-8, p 87-9, 96; 4-9, p 97-8, 106; 5-1, p 1-6; 5-2, p 27-8, 30, 33-4; 5-3, p 35-6, 41-2; 5-4, p 43-4. Queries: 4-6, p 68-9; 4-7, p 84-5; 4-8, p 94-5; 4-9, p 101-3; 5-2, p 30-32; 5-3, p 39-40; 5-4, p 44-5, 52. Index to queries in Vol. 4: 4-9, p 103-6.

STI - STIRPES: Texas State Genealogical Society Quarterly, published by the Society, 2528 University Drive South, Fort Worth 9, Texas. Editor: Edna Perry Deckler. Quarterly (Mar.): Vol. 2, 1962. $5.00 membership includes magazine; $6.00 by subscription, $1.50 per issue ($1.25 to members). Pages per issue: 35 to 40. Size of page: 6x9". Paper cover; saddle stitched. Society news, membership lists, etc.: 2-1, p 1, 10, 12, 28, 38-40; 2-2, p 41, 64, 69-72; 2-3, p 78-81, 104-9, 113; 2-4, p 117, 130, 136-151. Queries: 2-1, p 33-5 (Correction to Query # B1-18, p 35; see 2-4, p 149): 2-2, p 73-5; 2-3, p 114-115; 2-4, p 152.

SUP - Supplement to Ancestral Notes from Chedwato: See AN - ANCESTRAL NOTES

TAG - THE AMERICAN GENEALOGIST, published & edited by Donald Lines Jacobus, Box 3022, Westville Station, New Haven 15, Conn. Quarterly (Jan.): Vol. 38, 1962. $6.00 per vol., $2.00 per issue. Pages per issue: 64. Size of page: 6x9". Heavy paper cover, saddle stitched. Full name Index to Vol. 38 bound in Oct. issue, #4, p 257-85. Notes: 38-1, p 63-4; 38-3, p 170; 38-4, p 256. Queries: 38-2, p 89, 99, 113; 38-3, p 139, 163; 38-4, p 211, 219, 228, 242-3.

TS - THE TREESEARCHERS, published by the Southwest Kansas Genealogical Society, Rt. 2, Dodge City, Kansas. Editor: Ida Ellen Rath. Quarterly (Jan.): Vol. 4, 1962. $2.50 per year, $.50 per issue, $.50 for directory issue. Pages per issue: 16. Size of page: 8½x11". Printed binder cover provided with each vol. Notes, membership lists, accessions, etc.: 4-1, p 1-8, 10, 12, 16; 4-2, p 50-5, 58, 65; 4-3, p 66-71, 77-80, 83; 4-4, p 84, 86, 89, 93-5, 99. Directory of Surnames: 4-1, p 17-49. Queries: 4-1, p 13-15; 4-2, p 61-4; 4-3, p 81-2; 4-4, p 96-8. Correction (to Oct. 1961): 4-1, p 12.

TT - TREE TALKS, published by the Central New York Genealogical Society, 304 Briarcliffe Rd., Syracuse 14, N. Y. Editor: Mrs. Lester F. Myers. Quarterly (Mar.): Vol. 2, 1962. $3.75 per year; includes annual "Cousin Huntin'," published in Dec. (surname-query index), 44 pages in 1962. Pages per issue: 22 to 28. Size of page: 8½x11". No separate cover; punched for binder. Pages can be rearranged by county. Society news, book notices, etc.: 2-1, p 1-3; 2-2, p 16-19; 2-3, p 37-9; 2-4, p 59-63.

VA - THE VIRGINIA MAGAZINE OF HISTORY AND BIOGRAPHY, published by the Virginia Historical Society, 428 North Boulevard, Richmond 20, Va. Editor: William M. E. Rachel. Quarterly (Jan.): Vol. 70, 1962. $6.00 per year, $2.00 per issue. Pages per issue: 120 to 132. Size of page: 7x10". Heavy paper cover; bound. Full name index (32 pages in 1962) as separate publication, included with subscription. Material of genealogical interest only included in GPA INDEX 1962.

VG - THE VIRGINIA GENEALOGIST, published & edited by John Frederick Dorman, Box 4883, Washington 8, D. C. Quarterly (Jan.): Vol. 6, 1962. $5.00 per vol., $1.50 per issue. Pages per issue: 48. Size of page: 6x9". Heavy paper cover; saddle stitched. Full name Index (53 pages in 1962) bound in Oct. issue (#4). Editor's Page: 6-2, p 50; 6-3, p 98, 133-4; 6-4, p 146. Queries: 6-1, p 44-8; 6-2, p 88-96; 6-3, p 140-4; 6-4, p 183-4. Corrections & Comments: 6-1, p 27; 6-2, p 82.

VGA - THE VIRGINIA GAZETTE, published by The Virginia Gazette, Inc., Williamsburg, Va. Editor: John O. W. Gravely, III. Weekly (Friday) newspaper: $3.50 per year. Each issue contains column "Genealogy," edited by Dorothy Ford Wulfeck, 51 Park Ave., Naugatuck, Conn., which consists of queries and answers pertaining mostly to Va. families, book reviews & notices, occasional long articles, ads, etc.

WIS - NEWSLETTER: WISCONSIN STATE GENEALOGICAL SOCIETY, published by the Society. Editor: Walter L. Van Brocklin, 3064 S. 60th St., Apt. #3, Milwaukee 19, Wis. Three times a year (Sept., Jan., May): Vol. 8 #2, Jan. 1962; Vol. 9 #1, Sept. 1962. $1.00 per year, $.35 per issue. Pages per issue: 8 to 12. Size of page: 8½x11". No separate cover; stapled. Society news, announcements: 8-2, p 1-4, 7-8; 8-3, p 1-4, 10; 9-1, p 1-2, 4-6, 11. Queries: 8-2, p 4-7; 8-3, p 4-9; 9-1, p 6-11.

WM - WILLIAM & MARY QUARTERLY, published by the Institute of Early American History & Culture, Box 220, Williamsburg, Va. Quarterly (Jan.): Vol. 19 (3rd Series), 1962. $5.00 per year. Material of genealogical interest only is included in the GPA INDEX 1962.

WQ - GENEALOGIST'S WEEKLY QUERY INDEX, published by Meredith Grant Benner, P. O. Box 446, Casey, Ill. Fortnightly: $5.95 per year. Also published: INDEX TO THE HARTFORD TIMES, fortnightly: $5.95 per year. Both publications @ $9.95 per year. Size of page: 8½x11". Both are individual name indexes of names appearing in the query section of current genealogical publications and in the genealogical section of the Hartford Times.

YFT - YOUR FAMILY TREE, published & edited by Frances Strong Helman, 1082 Maple St., Indiana, Pa. Irregular date of issue: Vol. 10 # 3&4 (double issue), July 1962; Vol. 11#1, Dec. 1962. Subscription by vol. only; $4.00 per vol.; 120 pages in each vol. Back issues by vol. only. Pages per issue: 30. Size of page: 8½x11". Paper cover; stapled. Surname Index to Vol. 10, included in 10-3&4, pages 111-22. Notes, ads, etc.: 10-3&4, p 95, 109-10; 11-1, p 9, 30, inside back covers. Queries: 10-3&4, p 106-10; 11-1, p 27-30.

YY - YESTERYEARS, published & edited by Francis V. Grifone, Scipio Center, N. Y. Quarterly (Sept.): Vol. 5 # 19, March 1962: Vol. 6 #21, Sept. 1962. $3.00 per year, $5.50 for 2 years, $7.50 for 3 years. $1.00 per issue. Pages per issue: about 60. Size of page: 5½x8½". Stiff cover; saddle stitched. Illustrations. Index of surnames in issues: last two pages in 5-20, 5-21 and 5-22.

Periodicals listed on pages 1 to 12 include publications containing material of interest to genealogists as well as periodicals primarily concerned with genealogy.

GENEALOGICAL PERIODICAL ANNUAL INDEX

(Alabama, continued)
p 179-83

Ala., Covington Co. 1850 Census Schedule (by Mrs. B. W. Gandrud) ALA 4-2, p 66-75; 4-3, p 120-30

Ala., Covington Co. Bible Records. (+Beck, Wasdin, Beesley, Beasley, Bonham, Moore, Futch, Liles) (by Ruby Bryan) ALA 4-2, p 80-2

Ala., Covington Co. See Ala., Conecuh Co.

Ala., Crenshaw Co. See Ala., Conecuh Co.

Ala., Dallas Co. Deed Book A (by Flora England) ALA 4-4, p 197-9

Ala., Dallas Co. Obituaries (from the Selma, Ala., Free Press (by Frances Hailes) ALA 4-3, p 136-7

Ala., Hale Co. Bible Records (+Duskin, Johnston, Martin, Penn, Moore, Atkin, Clements, Parker, Parrish, Latta) (by Henry Poellnitz Johnston) ALA 4-3, p 117-9

Ala., Henry Co. Marriage Records, 1821-1871. ALA 4-1, p 4-11; 4-2, p 52-65; 4-3, p 104-116; 4-4, p 152-63

Ala., Jackson Co. Tombstone Inscriptions (Old Belefonte Cem., with notes on Martin family) (by Grace H. Puryear) ALA 4-3, p 131-3

Ala., Lawrence Co. See Va., vital rec.

Ala., Lee Co. Tombstone Inscriptions (Liberty Baptist Church) (by Mrs. W.V. Parker & Mrs. Grady Loftin, ALA 4-2, p76-9

Ala., Madison Co. 1830 Census (with notes on formation, etc.) (by Pauline Jones Gandrud) SGX 3-24, p 19-30

Ala., Marengo Co. Tombstone Inscriptions (Faunsdale, Ala.) (by Mrs. Nelle Morris Jenkins) ALA 4-4, p 184-7

Ala., Morgan Co. See Va., vital records

Ala., Perry Co. 1830 Census (Pauline Gandrud) SGX 3-22, p 43-7

Ala., Perry Co. 1850 Census Schedule (cont. from Sept. 1961 issue) ALA 4-1, p 27-36

Ala., Sumter Co. Orphans Book I (by Nell Motes Goggans) ALA 4-3, p 102-3

Ala., Sumter Co. 1850 Mortuary Schedule ALA 4-1, p 22-3

Ala., Tuscaloosa Co. Tombstone Inscriptions (Suddeth Cem., Gates Cem., Bryce Hospital Cem., McAddory Cem.) (by B. S. Hendrix, Jr.) ALA 4-3, p 134-5

(Alabama, continued)

Alabama. See also Tex., Navarro Co.

Alberty Family Notes (by Mrs. Richard Bland Turner) AFH 1-3, p 45-6

Alden-Pabodie Rouse. SEA 11-5, p 133

Aldrich. See Millard; Wyatt

Alexander, Katherine. See Calif., Sutter Creek

Alexander Cemetery (near Moody, Tex.) (by Mrs. J. Staton & Mrs. R. G. Murrie) BCT 5-3, p 4

Allard. See Horner

Allbright. See Bodine

Allday. See Knight

Allen, Cameron. See Anderson; Burton; Stovall

Allen, Mrs. H. P. See N.Y., Petersburg

Allen, Oliver E. See Lewis

Allen (Mass.) ML #3, p 44

Allen-Holt (1850 Census, Windsor Co., Vt.) AN 9-4, p 95

Allen-Robinson (Conn.) ML #4, p 71

Allen-Vaughan Bible Record. SUP #3, p 31

Allen. Bible Record (Allen, Mayer, Veach) (by Mrs. C. G. Garrett) TS 4-3, p 72-3

Allen. See Blood; Conant; Dunbar; Hammond; Payne; Pritchard; Saunders

Allensworth. See Sullivan

Allis. See Brownson

Allman, Mrs. Frederick Lee. See Willett

Allred. See Tex.

Allsup. See Easley

Almy. See R. I., Little Compton

Alrichs of New Castle, Delaware (+Humphries, Dilworth) (by Lewis D. Cook) See also Addenda, TAG 38-4, p 256. TAG 38-1, p 31-9; 38-2, p 90-9

Alsbee. See Cole

Alston. See Edwards

Alvord. See Crouch

Ames. See Davis; Smith

Amesbury. See Millard

Anderson, Bessie. See Poems & Songs

Anderson, Mrs. R. C. See Wick

Anderson-Herbert-Wynne: A Correction; And a Further Wynne Descent through the Wyatt & Twitty Families (+Hawkins, Rooker) (by Cameron Allen) TAG 38-1, p 13-19

Aylett. The Aylett Letters (1658-1676) & Other Aylett Papers (Evelyn Crady Adams) FC 36-1, p 64-5

Babcock. See Bodine
Bachelour. See "Welcome"
Bachman. A Letter from Rev. John Bachman, London, 1838 (of Charleston, S. C.) SCH 63-4, p 211-13
Bachman. See Kroll
Backus. See Baker
Bacon. See Page; Smith
Baer, Mrs. Frank L. See Hilts
Baer, Mabel Van Dyke. See Blaisdell; Ferguson; Grover; Havens
Bailey, Virginia G. See Ga., Burke Co.
Bailey, Rosalie Fellows. See Lloyd
Bailey. See Acklin
Baird. See Acklin; Schenck
Baker, Mrs. Wilson L. See Haynes
Baker. Will of Nathaniel Baker (Rensselaer Co., N. Y., 1839) (by Mrs. A. Santos) AN 9-3, p 57-8
Baker. The Bakers & Backuses of Canterbury, Conn. Who Moved to Granville, N. Y. (by John G. Hunt) DS 25-4, p 141-6
Baker-Beach Bible Record. FGQ 4-1, p 7
Baker-Brooks (Mass.) ML #1, p 11
Baker. Correction (to Vol. 24, p 142-5) DS 26-2, p 84
Baker. See Adams; Sholes; Tayloe
Balcom. From a Balcom Bible (by Mrs. M. I. Schrontz) DS 26-1, p 4
Baldinger, Nancy Shepard. See Wright
Baldridge, J. S. See Tex., Gonzales Co.
Baldwin, Dr. Jonas C. See N. Y., Onondaga Co.
Baldwin (1850 census, Essex Co., N. J.) ML #2, p 34
Baldwin (1850 Census, Essex Co., N.J.) ML #1, p 19
Baldwin-Sabins-Sabin (1870 Census, Tompkins Co., N. Y. ML #5, p 90-1
Baldwin. See Acklin
Ballard-Huston (Mass., Mich., Calif.) ML #3, p 59
Ballard. See Iowa, Pottawattomie Co.
Ballenger. See Dodd
Ballou. See Millard
Banks. William Banks Family Bible Record, in Middleburgh Records (N. Y.) (by Frances B. Spencer) YY 6-22, p 60-1
Banning. See Watkins
Barber, Connecticut & Luzerne Co., Co., Pa. (by George E. McCracken) TAG 38-1, p 64
Barber. See "Welcome"; Williams
Barbour, Philip L. See Kendall
Barclay, Mrs. John E. See Hinds Staples; Stockbridge
Barclay, Rachel E. See Faunce
Bargar, B. D. See S. C., Charles Town
Barker. Family Bible Record of George W. Barker of Youngstown, N. Y. & Mary H. Greenfield of Lewistown, N. Y. (by Mrs. M. E. Marsh, Jr.) DAR 96-1, p 37
Barker. See Cole; Cornman; Lively
Barlow, Lundie W. See Barlow; Foreign Genealogy; Heraldry
Barlow. The Barlow Family of England & Virginia: A Chain of Evidence, 1592-1659 (+Parker, Ellsey (Elzy), Hicks) (by Lundie W. Barlow) NGS 50-2, p 114-5
Barlow. See Acklin
Barnes-Barns (Leicester, Mass.) ML #4, p 68
Barnes Bible Records (+McAnderson, Graham, Tenant, McEwen, Guthrie) OGS 2-3, p 3
Barnes. See Ala., Clarke Co.; Brownson; Campbell; Houts
Barnett-Burton (1850 Census, Montgomery Co., Va. ML #1, p 19
Barnett. See Hewitt; Texas
Barns. See Barnes
Barnum-Gillette-Rinehart Bible Records (by Kathleen Common Schmidt) DS 25-4, p 173-4
Barrett. See Jones
Barroll, L. Wethered. See Md., Kent Co.
Barrows. See Acklin
Bartholme. See Flack
Bartholomew. See Millard; Patton
Bartholow-Lakin (Md.,Pa.) AN 9-1, p17
Bartholow. See Flack
Bartlett Family: Corrections (Mrs. Harry W. Rowe) NE July, p 230
Bartlett. See Smith
Barton. See Clay; Little
Bass, Una L. See Kelly
Bass. See Stevens
Bassett. See Conant
Batchelor-Sanford (N. Y., Tex.) ML #2,

(Bishop, continued)
Bishop-Ramsey (Va., Pa., Ohio) ML #3, p 50
Bishop. See Jackson; Shaw; Williams; Wilson
Bishopp Bible (by Mrs. E. R. Hutcherson) KCG 3-2, p 13-14
Bissell. See Morgan
Blackman Bible Record (+Wood) (by Harold Blackmun) SUP #3, p 25
Blackmun, Harold. See Blackman
Blair. See Scott
Blaisdell, Rev. Pension & Bounty Land Warrant for Isaac Blaisdell (Abigail Pettingill) (N. H.) (by Mabel Van Dyke Baer) AN 9-4, p 73-4
Blake (1870 Census, New Haven Co., Conn.) AN 9-3, p 64
Blake Coat-of-Arms (with family data) (by Hazel Kraft Eilers) HO 67-2, p 126-7
Blaker, Mrs. Anson. See Conant; Van Eaton
Blanchard. See Perry
Blocker. See Franks
Blood Family Bible (+Allen, Bryant) (by Phyllis Leach) OR 3-4, p 175
Blood. See Chamberlain
Blount, Mrs. Guy A. See Tex., Houston
Bock, Mrs. Eugene. See Justice; West
Bodge. See Methods, general
Bodine-Van Doren Bible Record. SUP #5 p 60
Bodine. The William Bodine Bible Record (+Babcock, Allbright) (by Mrs. Charles Horman) DS 25-4, p 173
Bogert. See Stoothoff
Boland. See Acklin
Bonham. See Ala., Covington Co.
Bonsack. See Plaine
Bonum. See Holmes
Booker, Origin of John Booker of York, Me. (Myrta Booker Robinson) NE Apr., p 89-90
Boone. Daniel Boone's Rifle Fired KG 4-2, p 47
Boone. See Karn; Ky., Daviess Co.
Bootes, Mrs. Fenton E. See N. Y., Yates Co. ; Francisco
Bootes, Thelma Burton. See Bootes
Bootes, Lineage of Ronnie Leigh Bootes (+Spencer, Briggs, Andrews, Burton,

(Bootes, continued)
Warner, Montague, Wightman, Vaughn) (by Thelma Burton Bootes) YY 5-20, p 198-201
Booth, Arthur. See Hewitt; Mich., Wayne Co.
Borders, Rev. Pensions: Peter Borders (Va.), p 22; Adam Boston (Bosteyon) (Va.), p 21-2; Andrew Boston (N. C.) p 22; Frederick Boyer (Pa.), p 22; John Godlieb Boyer (Md.), p 22-3 AN 9-1
Borders. See Grover
Borland Coat-of-Arms (with family data) (by Hazel Kraft Eilers) HO 67-9, p 124, 126-7, 129
Boroughs. See Ala., Clarke Co.
Borrum, James L. See Jopling; Tenn., Purdy
Borum, Family Bible Records (+Borum, Broom, Cleave, Conner, Day, Marley, Dickason, Murrell, Verser, Neilson) AUS 3-4, p 162-3
Boss. See Acklin; Beavers
Boster-Kerns (1850 Census, Gallia Co., Ohio) ML #3, p 57
Boster, Civil War Pensions: Harrison Boster (Iowa), p 63; Wallace W. Thorp (N. Y.), p 69 in SUP #6
Boster, Gallia Co., Ohio, Marriage Records (all Boster) AN 9-3, p 59
Boster. See Clare
Bosteyon. See Borders
Bostick, Raymond H. See Lewallen
Bostick, Raymond Harrison. See Bostick
Bostick Family Records (by Raymond Harrison Bostick) OH 4-1, p 16-18
Boston, Earl R. See Ind., Washington Co.
Boston, Mrs. Earl R. See Ind., Washington Co.
Boston. See Borders
Boutell. See Hewitt
Boutelle. See Grover
Bowdish-Lawton Bible Record (Noel C. Stevenson) POR 12-3, p 23
Bowditch, Harold. See Hartwell
Bowen. See Millard; Smith
Bower (1850 Census, Harrison Co., Ohio) ML #5, p 98

(Bower, continued)
Bower. See Bauer
Bowers. See Grover
Bowman, Mrs. Lewis O. See Sources, family associations
Bowman. See Kitchin
Bowra, Bernice Gardner. See N.M., San Juan Co.
Boyce. See Millard
Boyd. See Marvel; McPherson; Roberds
Boyd, Janice. See Conn., East Haddam
Boyer. See Borders
Boyes. See Lively
Boyesen, Mrs. J. W. See Vt., Franklin Co.
Boyle, Mrs. Bernard Samuel. See Reynolds
Boyle. See McBride
Boynton (Mass.) ML #2, p 27
Boynton-Jewett-Beaman (Mass., Vt.) ML #1, p 10
Bradford. See Adams
Bradley. See Acklin; Rider; Tayloe
Bradley-Howard-Hill Bible Record SUP #5, p 54-5
Bradly. See Peck
Bradt-Swart (1855 Census, Schenectady Co., N. Y.) ML #3, p 46
Bradway. See Asay
Bragdon, Lester MacKenzie. See Maine, York
Brainard-Andrews (N. Y., Ill.) ML #4, p 74-5
Brainard-Crosby (Conn., N. Y., Ill.) ML #3, p 59
Brainard. See Crosby
Brainerd. See Goff
Braley. See Vt., Windham Co.
Braman Bible Record. SUP #1, p 7-8
Bran. See Millard
Brandbery. See Franks
Brandebury & Beiter Bible Records (+Hamilton, Besore) OGS 2-4, p 4
Brant, Jacob. See Zimmerman
Braun, A "Hessian Soldier" in Lexington, Ky. (by Marie Dickore) FC 36-2, p 184-5
Bray. See Grover
Brayton, Isabella Weir. See N. Y., Hartford
Brayton. See N. Y., Hartford
Breckinridge, Attorney General John

(Breckinridge, continued)
Breckinridge (by Lowell H. Harrison) FC 36-4, p 319-28
Breijandt. See Bryant
Breneman-Holmes (deeds in Lancaster Co., Pa. & Washington Co., Iowa) AN 9-6, p 128-30
Brent, The Catholic Brents of Colonial Virginia: An Instance of Practical Toleration (by Bruce E. Steiner) VA 70-4, p 387-409
Brent, (Abstracts of Brent Wills, Lancaster Co., Va., in "Brentwood & the Brents") (by James C. Wilfong, Jr.) CSM, 10-3, p 247-53
Brevard. See Tayloe
Breyant. See Bryant
Brians. See Bryant
Briant (1860 Census, Independence Co., Ark.) ML #1, p 3
Briant. See Bryant
Bridgers, Frank E. See Sources, libraries
Bridges, Gorham. (A 1913 Obituary) (by Jean Pardue) POR 11-6, p 46
Brien. See Franklin
Briggs, The Identity of Susannah, Second Wife of John (3) Briggs of East Greenwich, R. I. (by Gerald James Parsons) (+Peirce, Spencer) TAG 38-2, p 83-4
Briggs. See Bootes; Place; R. I., Little Compton; N. Y., Hartford
Brinson. See McFarland
Bristol, Edwin L. See N. Y., Ontario Co.
Britton. See Tenn., Anderson Co.
Britz, Deanna. See Parrish
Brock. See Bearden
Brockman Bible Record (by Vella Good) HG 2-1, p 4
Brodock. See N. Y., Oneida Co.
Bromfield, Louis Bromfield's Genealogy OGS 2-2, p 3
Bronn (Brown) Bible Record (+Daniels, Irish, Mainer) SUP #1, p 1-2
Bronson. See Brownson
Brookes. See Hickson
Brooks-McKaughan (Tenn., Tex.) ML #2, p 26
Brooks-Ward-Chamberlain-Rogers Bible Record. SUP #1, p 4-6

Cartwright, Olive Hotchkiss. See Olive
Cary. William Cary Family Bible Record, in Middleburgh Records (N. Y.) (+Cook, Sweet, Southwick, Hammond, Merritt, Devol (?), Fowler, Dillingham, Jackson) (by Frances B. Spencer) YY 6-22, p 62-4
Case. Two Case Bible Records (+Wilbur, Tompkins) (by Benjamin Franklin Wilbour) NE Oct., p 283-4
Case Bible Records (+Montigue) SUP #1, p 8-9
Case Correction (referring to Case article, TAG Vol. 34, p 66) TAG 38-3, p 183
Case. See Montigue; Rathbun
Cason. Bible Record of Adelaide Louise Lampton Cason (+Lampton) (by Lula C. Kainer) KG 4-1, p 13-15
Casper-Eubank Bible Record (Lowell DeMoss) MI 8-4, p 7
Casteel. See Cameron
Castel. See Harper
Castlen. See Prosser
Castner. See Richardson
Cate, Mrs. Margaret Davis Cate. Obituary. NGS 50-2, p 119-20
Catlin. See Smead
Cave. See Smith
Cavendish (1850 Census, Windson Co., Vt.) ML #4, p 76
Caywood. A Soldier of 1812 & His Bounty Land (Records of William Caywood) (+Walker, Ennis) (by Minnie Dubbs Millbrook) DS 26-1, p 39
Census records. See Sources, census. See also individual state & county
Chadwick. A Letter from a Civil War Sailor. FGQ 4-4, p 64-5
Chadwick-Ellis Bible Record. SUP #5, p 58-9
Chamberlain Family Records (+Morgan, Sommes, Taylor, Swan, Druse, Newell, Rundle, Martindale, White, Blood) (by Prentiss Glazier) NYR 93-1, p 10-13
Chamberlain. See Brooks
Champion. Ella Champion: A Biography in "Pioneer Women Teachers of Michigan" (Margaret Mullin & Margery North) MH 3-4, p 191-4
Champion Bible Record (by Noel C. Stevenson) POR 11-10, p 79
Chancy. See Sparkman
Chandler. See Hays
Chapman. Inscriptions from Chapman Cemetery at Bellevue, Giles Co., Va. (+Pendleton) AN 9-3, p 60-1
Chapman. Inbreeding in a Chapman Family (+Rollins) (by Mrs. Harold C. Pickwick & Thomas H. Roderick) TAG 38-4, p 240-2
Chapman. See Brown; Utah, Davis Co.
Chapple. See Drury
Charles-Anderson (N. C., Ind.) ML #3, p 45
Charlton. See Bearden
Chase, Mary Henrietta. See Seeley
Chase, Lewis Fifield. Obituary DS 25-3, p 96
Chase. Notes on Chase & Kezer Families (+Keeser, Moore, Green, Cole, Spaulding, McPherson, Buckstaff, Kane, Farrell, Farrow, Johnson, Judd, Rogers, Davis, Merriam, Hitchings, Worrell, Saunders) (by Mrs. James D. McGlynn) DS 25-3, p 97-102
Chase-Holcomb Bible Record SUP #1, p 6-7
Chase. See Millard
Chatham-Shade Bible Record (+Burtleps, Weir, etc.) SUP #5, p 49-50
Chauncey. See Adams
Chenie. See Hamtramck
Chick. See Burleigh
N.B. Chichester: See Lloyd
Chiles-Regnholz Bible Record (by Noel C. Stevenson) POR 12-2, p 15
Chilton. Origin of the Chiltons of The Mayflower (John G. Hunt) TAG 38-4, p 244-5
China. See Foreign Genealogy
Chindgren. See Hult
Chitwood. See Elswick
Christopher, Adrienne. See Kans., vital statistics
Chubo. See Collins
Civil War. See Military records
Claiborne Coat-of-Arms (with family data (by Hazel Kraft Eilers) HO 66-11, p 126-7
Clare-Kenton-Boster (1850 Census, Montgomery Co., Va.) ML #1, p 18
Clark, Bertha W. See Holmes
Clark, Mrs. Fred A., Jr. See Lull
Clark, Capt. Henry O. See Mo., military records

Clark, Raymond B., Jr. See Md., sources, Baltimore Co., Kent Co., St. Mary's Co., Talbot Co.; Methods, general

Clark, Sara Seth. See Md., Baltimore Co., Kent Co., Talbot Co.

Clark Bible Record (+Cutter) (by Noel C. Stevenson) POR 11-6, p 47

Clark Bible Record (Washington Co., Pa.) SUP #1, p 11-12

Clark-Colegrove Bible Record. SUP #3, p 30

Clark-Eaton (Mass.) AN 9-4, p 86

Clark-Eddy-Sprague Connections, Rhode Island (by Barbara B. McGee) TAG 38-2, p 113

Clark. Revolutionary Patriot, No. 4: Gershom Clark. SEA 12-3, p 215

Clark. See Adams; Austin; Ferguson; Hart; Howe; Ky., Muhlenberg Co.; Sanford

Clarke. See Ky., Muhlenberg Co.; Methods, general; N. Y., Otsego Co.

Clason. See Dan

Class Family Records (+Theiler, Slappey, Arthur, Snyder) (by Louise K. Crowder) SGX 3-21, p 13-14

Clause. See Cornman

Clay-Cook Family Bible (+High, Barton, Thomas) (by Mrs. Alexander Pratt) VG 6-3, p 130-1

Clayton. See Dennis

Cleave. See Borum

Cleaveland Bible Record, in Middleburgh Records (N. Y.) (+Galusha) (Frances B. Spencer) YY 6-22, p 59

Cleaveland. See Hewitt

Clement. William Clement Family Bible Record, in Middleburgh Records (N.Y. (+Porter, Millspaugh) (Frances B. Spencer) YY 6-22, p 60

Clement. See Thorne

Clements. See Ala., Hale Co.

Clemmons. See Tex., Austin Co.

Cleveland. See Ala., Clarke Co.; Hewitt; Tex., Austin Co.

Clifford. See Acklin

Clift, G. Glenn. See Ky., military records

Clift. Bible Record Corrections (+Clift, Penland) (by Gladys Gaston) KCG 2-11, p 8

Cline, Mrs. Frank. See Ark., Montgomery Co.

Clogston. See Morrison

Clopper. See Millard

Clough, Mrs. P. W. See Ky., Harrison Co.

Cobb. The Two Howell Cobbs: A Case of Mistaken Identity (by Horace Montgomery) JSH 28-3, p 348-55

Cobb. A Cobb Bible Record (+Nurse) (by Mrs. James B. Fish) DS 26-1, p 38

Cobb. See Millard

Cochran. See Payne

Cockrell, Mrs. James Knox. See Engle

Coddington, John Insley. See Brownson; Gregory; Howard; Nutt; Singletary; Stoothoff; Wilton

Coddington. See Nevins; Stoothoff

Codebeck. See N. Y., Orange Co.

Coffin, Sarah Adams. See N. Y., Onondaga Co.

Cogswell. See Wellington

Cole-Bryant Bible Record. SUP #5, p59-60

Cole-Barker-Hardy-Knight-Alsbee (Mass., N. H.) ML #1, p 12-13

Cole. See Chase; Hanson; Place; Welsh

Colegrove. See Clark; Millard

Coleman, Daniel. See Coleman

Coleman, Dorothy S. See Quizzes, cartoons, etc.

Coleman Family (Daniel Coleman) SGX 3-23, p 37-8

Coleman-Owings Article from The Rockwood Times (Rockwood, Tenn.) (+Owens, Sumpter) (by Mrs. E. R. Hutcherson) KCG 2-13, p 7-8

Colfax Family Data NJG 9-4, p 382

Colgin Note (answer to query) MGX 1&2, p 39-40

Colket, Meredith B. See Sources, publications

Collamer, Mrs. Newton L. Obituary. NGS 50-2, p 119

Collins, Mrs. C. C. See Ind., Putnam Co.

Collins. See Marvel

Collins-Chubo (Vt., Conn., N. Y.) AN 9-6, p 125

Collins. See Franks; N. Y., Lewis Co.

Colorado. Gold Is Where You Find It (source material at Colo. State Hist. Society Library) (by Laura Allyn Ekstrom) CG 23-2, p 48-9

Colorado. Early Colorado Marriages

(Colorado, continued)
(Dec. 1878 to Jan. 28, 1879) (Cont. from Vol. 22, p 105) CG 23-1, p 21-2; 23-2, p 53; 23-4, p 98-9
Colo., Arapahoe Co. Probate Records CG 23-1, p 13-14
Colo., Denver. Burial Records of Calvary Cemetery (cont. from Vol. 22, p 115) CG 23-1, p 23-4; 23-3, p 74-75; 23-4, p 113
Colsher. See Eveland
Colson-Goldie Notes (N.Y., Kansas, Okla) OKL 7-3, p 318
Colton. See Kelting
Colwell. See Callaway
Combs. Family Record of Gilbert Combs (+Denton) (Winifred Lovering Holman) NGS 50-1, p 48-9
Comer. See Winter
Comstock (1850 Census, Herkimer Co., N. Y.) ML #1, p 18
Comstock-Fanning-Bennett-Ash (R. I., N. Y.) ML #1, p 14
Comstock. See Bennett; Conant; Smith; Stebbins
Conant Family Bible Records (+Allen, Parmenter, Comstock, Robbins, Loveland, Lillibridge, Bassett, Rathbon) (by Mrs. Anson Blaker) SEA 11-8, p 159
Condit, Aaron. See N. J., Hanover
Confederate records. See Military records
Confederate Veterans Magazine. See Military records
Congar. See Conger
Conger, Hiram G. See Conger
Conger-Congar-Koniger Bible Records (+Kelly, Beaman, Pierson, Baxter) (by Hiram G. Conger) NJG 9-4, p 385
Conklin. See Hull
Connecticut, East Haddam. Millington Church Records (Janice Boyd) AN 9-6, p 124
Conn., New London Co. (Norwich) Petition of Men of Norwich...for a Military Company...1775; Pay Roll for same, 1776, & Order for duty, 1776. DAR 96-11, p 710
Conn., Norwich. Second Congregational Church Records (Chelsea Church) AN 9-1, p 9-13

(Connecticut, continued)
Conn., Sharon. Probate Records (+Hart, Ketcham, Spencer, Davis, Lord) AN 9-4, p 80-1
Conn., Sharon. Vital Records AN 9-2, p 32-3
Connelly. John Connelly of Boone Co. Mo., Rev. War Pension Applicant (brief note) SEA 12-3, p 215
Conner. See Borum; Harris; Shannon
Conover. See Hilts. See also correction notice in NYR listing, p 8, GPA INDEX, 1962
Converse. See Covil
Cook, Lewis D. See Alrichs
Cook (1850 Census, Montgomery Co., Ind.) ML #2, p 39
Cook (1850 Census of Washington Co., Ky., & of Platte Co., Mo.) ML #1, p 6
Cook (1850 Census, Cole Co., Mo.) ML #2, p 39
Cook. Rev. Pension Records: Jesse Cook (Tenn. - with notes by Mrs. Alexander Pratt), p 122-4; Ebenezer Grover, p 128; Giles Thomas (Md., Va.), p 134-5; Joshua Harris (Mass., N. Y., Vt.), p 135. AN 9-6
Cook. Tombstone of Capt. B. F. Cook (Osceola, Mo.) (by Mrs. Dale Hursh) KCG 2-13, p 2
Cook. See Beavers; Cary; Clay; Gates; Preston; Prosser; Sparkman; Whyte
Cooley. Correction to Vol. 24, p 149-53: DS 25-3, p 96
Cooley. See Powers; Wood
Coombs. See Ga., Twiggs Co.
Coon- Tibbetts- Drake (1865 Census, Orleans Co., N. Y.) ML #2, p 40
Coons, Jessie. See N. Y., Yates Co.
Coons, Robert. See N. Y., Yates Co.
Cooper. See Rea
Corbin. See Hilling
Corey, Philip S. See King
Corliss, Mrs. George. See Taplin
Cornell. See Thorne
Cornish. See Payne
Cornman. The Family of John Cornman, Sugar Baker of Philadelphia (illustrated) (+Goos, Peter, Pawling, Ross, Ogden, Senneff, Clause,

(Ellis, continued)
Ellis. See Chadwick; Fitzsimmons; Millard
Ellsey (Elzy). See Barlow
Ellsworth. Ephraim Elmer Ellsworth: The Civil War & New York State (illus.) (by Henry Weber) YY 5-19, p 121-6
Elmendorf. See Wiest
Elswick. Family Records (Elswick-McClung-Richardson-Chitwood) (by Mrs. Howard G. Bennett) SGX 3-22, p 42
Elzy. See Barlow
Emach (1870 Census, New Haven Co., Conn.) AN 9-4, p 93
Emerson, Frances E. See Ind., Marshall Co.
Emerson, Rev. Warren. See Mass., vital records
Emerson. See Gates
Emigrants. Ship List of the "Orient", 19 May 1842 (by Lucy Mary Kellogg) DS 26-2, p 63-4
Emigrants. Advice to German Emigrants, 1749 (with notes on Melchior Family) (by Hannah Benner Roach) PGM 22-4, p 226-37
Emigrants. Some Emigrants to America from the Ludwigsburg Dist., Wurtemberg, Germany, 1738-1750 (many to Penn.) (by Paul W. Prindle) NYR 93-2, p 65-6
Emigrants. See also Sources, libraries; Foreign Genealogy
Emmell. See Voorhees
Emory. See Rogers
Enfinger, Doris G. See Fla.,Holmes Co.
England. See Foreign genealogy
England, Flora. See Ala., Dallas Co.
Engle-Greentree-Auerbach Note (by Mrs. James Knox Cockrell) NGS 50-2, p 73
Ennis. See Caywood
Enos. See Adams
Ernest. See Ernst
Ernst-Ernest (Adelle Bartlett Harper) GM, Vol. 5 (1962)
Esker, Katie-Prince Ward. See Montgomery
Estes Genealogy: Additions (+Pruitt) NE Oct., p 308-9
Estill, Mrs. Frank. See Military records
Eubank. See Casper
Evans, Charles F. H. See Mortimer
Evans, George C. See Decker
Evans, R. W. See Van Doren
Evans. See Tayloe
Eveland & Stull Family Bible Records (+Woolerer, Colsher, Ingalls, Griffith, Faulkrod) (by Hazel K. Eilers) NJG 10-1, p 395
Everett, Mrs. Robert C. Obituary SEA 11-9, p 173
Everett (by Adelle Bartlett Harper) GM, Vol. 5 (1962)
Everett Bible Records (Mrs. P. A. Lundblade) SEA 11-9, p 173-4
Everett. See Brownson
Everham, Virginia. See Mich., St. Clair Co.

Fairbairn, Charlotte Judd. See Harper
Fakes. See Moon
Falk. See Mich., Barry Co.
Family Associations. See Sources, publications; Sources, family associations
Family Reunions. See Sources, family associations
Fancher. See Patton
Fanning. See Comstock; Wight
Fant. See Belt
Farbank. See Hammond
Farnham, Charles William. See Smith
Farrar. See Yarberry
Farrell. See Chase
Farrer, Cornelia Hart. See Hart
Farrer, Mrs. Eugene. See Ida., Swan Lake
Farrington. See Millard
Farrow. See Chase
Farwell. See Drury
Faulk. See Ga., Twiggs Co.
Faulkrod. See Eveland
Faunce Family: Addenda & Corrections (by Rachel E. Barclay) NE July, p 188-91
Faunce. See Holmes
Feagin. See Ala., Conecuh Co.
Felt. See Smith
Fenno, Florence Ford. See N.Y.,Hartford

Ferguson, Nancy. See Va.
Ferguson. Dr. Richard Ferguson (1769-1853): Pioneer Surgeon of Louisville Attended Gen. George Rogers Clark (by Evelyn Crady Adams) FC 36-2, p 177-83
Ferguson. Civil War Pension of David S. Ferguson (Ohio) (by Mabel Van Dyke Baer) AN 9-6, p 131
Ferguson-Carpenter (1870 Census, Vernon Co., Wisc.) ML #2, p 39
Ferguson. See Ky., Muhlenberg Co.
Ferreira, A. L., Jr. See Klinefelter
Ferris. (Ferris notes in) Family Bible Records STA 5-3, p 41
Ferris. See Smith
Ferry. See Ruby
Field (Mass.) ML #3, p 47
Field. See Thorne
Fields, Mrs. C. E. See Sparkman
Fillmore. See Millard
Finch, Jean Haynes. See Haynes
Finch-Ogden (1850 Census, Alleghany Co., N. Y.) ML #1, p 9
Finn. See Millard
Finney-Atkinson Bible Record (by Noel C. Stevenson) POR 12-4, p 31
Fish, Mrs. James B. See Cobb
Fish-Brown Bible Record (G. G. Griffeth) DS 26-1, p 4
Fish. See Wood
Fisher, Mrs. Carl J. See Ind., military records
Fisher. See Morse
Fisk. See Richardson
Fiske. See Powers
Fitch. See Tayloe
Fitts. See Richardson
Fitzalan. See Foreign genealogy
Fitz Randolph. Capt. Nathaniel Fitz Randolph, 1747-1780, N. J. Revolutionary Hero NJG 9-3, p 367
Fitzsimmons, Ellis, Lee, Perkins, Radford, Redding & Allied Lines (cont. from Vol. 22, p 101) (with map in #2 & illus. in #3) (by Bernice FitzSimmons Hathaway) CG 23-2, p 31-43; 23-3, p 63-70
Flack-Bartholme (Bartholow) (Md.) AN 9-1, p 17
Flaherty. See Young
Fletcher. See Ore., Clackamas Co.
Flinn. See Ala., Clarke Co.; Flinn; Millard
Flood. See Brownson
Fla. Tories in Florida During Revolution SEA 12-2, p 205-6
Fla., vital records. Genealogical Items on Florida residents found in S. C. (and elsewhere) (Cont. from previous issue) (by Laura B. Jones) SGX 3-22, p 5-8
Fla., Alachua Co. Micanopy Cemetery (cont. from previous issue) (by Mrs. Henry Simpson) SGX 3-21, p 15-18
Fla., Duval Co. Probate Records, Series I (by Aurora C. Shaw) SGX 3-22, p 11-14; 3-23, p 19-24 (Series II); 3-24, p 7-12 (Series III)
Fla., Holmes Co. Old Smith Cemetery (Doris Gillman Enfinger) SGX 3-23, p 18
Fla., St. Augustine. Cemetery Records: Deceased of the Indian War (buried below Picolatti, near St. Augustine) SGX 3-21, p 14
Fluker. See Campbell
Flynn (Flinn) Bible Records (by Jean Pardue) SGX 3-23, p 46
Fogleman. See Shaw
Forbush, La Verne Hill. See Md.
Ford Note. NJG 9-3, p 371. See also correction in NJG 9-4, p 384
Foreign Genealogy.
Royal Ancestry of Joseph Bowles (correction to 37:115 - Despenser lineage) (by Walter Lee Sheppard, Jr., in "Errata & Addenda") TAG 38-3, p 180
A Hitherto Unnoted Descent from King Henry I (Walter Lee Sheppard, Jr.) NE Oct., p 278-80
An Interesting Lineage (Magna Carta Sureties) (by Blanche Dumanois) FGQ 4-2, p 30-5
Are You a Descendant of Lady Godiva? (by Walter Lee Sheppard, Jr.) NGS 50-2, p 74-8
The Early Harcourts (by Lundie W. Barlow) NE Apr., p 91-6
Dictionary of Scottish Emigrants (an announcement) (by Donald

Fritz. See Kieffer
Frost Bible Records (+Ake, Price) (by Mrs. A. B. Spencer, Jr.) ALA 4-4, p 188-91
Frost. See Hamtramck
Fry, Mrs. C. N. See Tex., Indianola
Fulgham Bible (+Taylor, Kirkwood) (by J. P. Landers) BCT 5-6, p 5-6
Fuller. See Delano; Francisco; Millard; Prince
Fulton. See Ky., Bardstown; Vanderburgh
Futch. See Ala., Covington Co.

Gable. See Spears
Gadsden. Christopher Gadsden: Radical or Conservative Revolutionary? (by Richard Walsh) SCH 63-4, p 195-203
Gailey, Leone Adkins. See Adkins
Galbraith. Col. Galbraith Was Early Justice (Bedford Co., Pa.) LM 3-2, p 7
Gallop. See Antill
Gallup. See Delano; Stark
Galusha. See Cleaveland
Gandrud, Mrs. B. W. See Ala., Covington Co.
Gandrud, Pauline Jones. See Ala., Madison Co., Perry Co.; Rodgers
Gardner, Charles Carroll. See N. J.; N. J., Cape May Co., Little Egg Harbor Twp., Mansfield Twp., New Hanover Twp., Northampton Twp.
Gardner, Martha Carnahan. See Methods, general
Gardner. See Millard
Gardener. See Nevins
Garfield. See Lamb
Garner, Mrs. Carl. See Tex., sources
Garretson. See Hanson
Garrett, Mrs. C. G. See Allen
Garrett, Mrs. C. J. See Ind., Military records
Garrett, Margaret Zeller. See Winegardner
Garrett, Tommie Attaway. See Jones
Garrett. Richard (1) Garrett (c 1615-1662) of Scituate, Mass. (by Maclean W. McLean) TAG 38-2, p 74-81
Garrett. See Jones
Garrison. Will of John Garrison (1796 -

(Garrison, continued)
Rensselaer Co., N. Y.) AN 9-3, p 58
Garwood (1850 Census, Burlington Co., N. J.) ML #5, p 97
Gaston, Gladys. See Clift
Gates Cemetery Inscriptions, Otego Co., N. Y. (Cook, Turner, Wilsey, Emerson) (by Stanley L. Moore) NE Apr., p 151-2
Gates. See Ala., Tuscaloosa Co.
Gatewood. See Sullivan
Gatton. See Ore., Multnomah Co.
Gay, Alemetta P. See Ill., Warren Co.
Gay. See Hewitt; Howe
Gaylord. See Brownson
Gehr (1850 Census, Crawford Co., Pa.) ML #1, p 4
Gentry, William R., Jr. See Gentry
Gentry. How to Rebury a Revolutionary Soldier (by William R. Gentry, Jr.) MHR 56-3, p 274-9
George, Suzanne Calhoun. See Tex., Navarro Co.
George, Mrs. Thomas McMillan. See Tex., Navarro Co.
George, Mrs. T. M. III. See Carroll; Tex., Navarro Co.
George-Warren (N. C., Ala.) ML #3, p 55
George. See Brown; Moyle
Georgia Genealogical Items (by Mrs. A. I. Richardson) Series IV: SGX 3-23, p 42-5; Series V: SGX 3-24, p 13-18
Georgia Research Material. STI 2-1, p 5
Ga., vital records. Miscellaneous Obituary Notes (primarily with Ga. connection - other states mentioned) (by Bernice Haworth) SGX 3-23, p 18
Ga., Burke Co. Slave Owners Within the First Assessment District of Burke Co., Ga., in 1798 - A Tax List (by Virginia Griffin Bailey) NGS 50-2, p 69-73
Ga., Elbert Co. (Muster Roll, State Militia, 1793; 1796 Pay Rolls) DAR 96-8, p 617-19
Ga., Fayette Co. Georgia Volunteers for Service in Texas Revolution

(Georgia, continued)
(from Fayette Co., Ga.) (by Mrs. A. B. Harmonson) STI 2-1, p 4-5
Ga., Jasper Co. 1850 Census (+Benton, Maddux) AN 9-6, p 144
Ga., Oglethorpe City Cemetery (partial listing) (by Jessie Alla James & Carol Shill) SGX 3-23, p 46
Ga., Tattnall Co. Marriages (by Mrs. A. I. Richardson) SGX 3-22, p 15-17
Ga., Twiggs Co. Cemetery Records (Vaughn Cem., Jeffersonville Cem., Ezekiel Wimberly Cem., Bryan Cem., Pace Cem., Crocker Cem., Faulk Cem., "Denson Level", Coombs Cem., Dye Cem. DAR 96-10, p 660-1. See correction in DAR 96-12, p 745: "Page 661, col. 2: Transfer description under "Faulk Cem." above astericks so that it applies to "Crocker Cem." Transfer description under "Denson Level" above astericks so that it applies to "Faulk Cem." Last two names in column 2 (Wm. Faulk & Virginia A. Faulk) should have the heading "Solomon-Faulk Cemetery." Description (of cem.) is on Page 745, Dec. Issue (96-12).
Ga., Wilkes Co. Marriages (by Mrs. A. I. Richardson) SGX 3-22, p 18-20
Ga., Wilkinson Co. Poplar Springs Cemetery DAR 96-10, p 660
Gerard. Thomas Gerard & His Sons-in-Law. (by Edwin W. Beitzell) CSM 10-10, p 300-306; 10-11, p 307-12
Germany. See Emigrants
Germond-Lowerre Bible Record (+Peters) SUP #3, p 35-6
Getty. James Getty of Ontario, Canada, & of Sanilac Co., Mich. (by Eva Murrell Harmison) DS 25-4, p 177
Gibbons. See Millard
Gibbs-Daniels Bible Record SUP #5, p 50-1
Gibbs. See Peck
Gibson-Wise (1840 Census, Stark Co., Ohio) ML #5, p 92
Gibson. See Rodgers
Giddings (New England) ML #1, p 7
Giffard. See Methods
Gifford. See Nevins; R. I., Little Compton
Gilbert. See Lightcap; Rodman
Giles, Mrs. Clarence. See Military records
Gillaspy. See Linkswiler
Gillett (1850 Census, Ashland Co., Ohio) AN 9-4, p 96
Gillett. See Griffin
Gillette. See Barnum
Gilliland Bible Records (+Harvey) MGX 8-1&2, p 20-1, 40
Gilman. See Platts
Gilmore. See McKinney; Millard
Gilpin. See Mendenhall
Gindrat. See Winter
Githens-Kughler (Pa., N. J.) AN 9-6, p 137-8
Glassgow-Hitchcock (Pa., Ohio) AN 9-6, p 138
Glazier, Prentiss. See Chamberlain
Glenn. See Ky., Muhlenberg Co.
Glover, Ruth Jernigan. See Military records
Glover. See Thorne
Goddard (Conn.) ML #5, p 96
Goddard-Arms (Quebec, Canada, & Mass.) ML #2, p 21
Godfrey, Robert. Ancestor Table (No. CIX) TAG 38-2, p 85-6
Godwin. See Sparkman
Goff-Brainerd-Rowley (Conn., N. Y., Canada) ML #5, p 95
Goff. See Millard
Goggans, Nell Motes. See Ala., Sumter Co.
Goldie. See Colson
Good, Vella. See Brockman
Goodell. See N. Y., Hartford
Goodspeed. See Winslow
Goos. See Cornman
Gorder. See Howe
Gordon. See Mercer
Goshow, Mildred. See Cornman
Graham, Gid. See Nomenclature
Graham, Ola Johnson. See Tenn., Henry Co.
Graham. See Barnes
Grandgent Family Bible Record (+Hall, Story, Mann) (by Jerold Story) TS 4-4, p 91-2
Grandgent (Pa.) ML #4, p 63
Grant-Summers (Ill., Tex.) ML #4, p 69-70

Graves, Alice M. See Ind., Lawrence Co.; N. C., Surry Co.
Graves. See Brownson; Ind., Lawrence Co.; Winslow
Gray-Hutchinson (Maine) ML #4, p 74
Gray. See Miss., Amite Co.; Stapp
Grayson. The Confederate Diary of William John Grayson (by Elmer L. Puryear) SCH 63-3, p 137-49; 63-4, p 214-26
Green, Mrs. Frank H. See Smith
Green Family of Penn. (+Sloan, Davis, Frazee, Friend) (by Alice D. Serrell) DS 26-2, p 49-50
Green. John Green Bible Records (+Jones) (by Lauretta Russell) SGX 3-21, p 30
Green (1850 Census, Chittenden Co., Vt.) AN 9-4, p 93
Green. Ebenezer Green, New York; Rev. War Pension (+Salisbury) (by Janis Miller) TT 2-3, p 40
Green. Jehiel Green, New York; Rev. War Pension Applicant (+Armstrong) (by Janis Miller) TT 2-4, p 64
Green. See Chase; Dan; Jackson; Kingsland; Postell; Sibley
Greenlief. See Merrill
Greentree. See Engle
Greer. Family Bible Record of Harry Greer & Mary Greer (by Mabel Greer McLeod) DAR 96-12, p 744
Gregg. See Tex., Austin
Gregory. Some Ancestors of Henry (1) Gregory: Worsley & Parr (by John Insley Coddington) TAG 38-3, p 171-4
Gregory. See Acklin
Gren, Axel Henry. Ancestor Table (No. CXI) See also Correction: 38-3, p 181. TAG 38-2, p 87-8
Griffeth, G. G. See Fish
Griffin, Inez H. See S. C., sources
Griffin. John Griffin of Windsor & Simsbury, Conn. (by George E. McCracken) (+Pond, Humphrey, Wilson, Gillett, Segar, Willcockson (Wilcoxson) TAG 38-2, p 100-112
Griffin. Family Bible Record of John Scarlett Griffin (Vicksburg, Miss.) (+Lane) (by Mrs. Lydia S. Griffin Trenholm) DAR 96-12, p 743
Griffith. See Eveland
Grinder. See Turnbow
Grindle-Sawyer (Mass.) ML #4, p 63
Griswold (1855 Census, Delaware Co., N. Y.) ML #1, p 5
Griswold (1850 Census, Lucas Co., Ohio) AN 9-2, p 47
Griswold-Johnson (1850 Census, Barrien Co., Mich., & Clayton Co., Iowa) ML #5, p 99
Griswold-Meacham-Osborn (Conn., N.Y) ML #3, p 51
Griswold. See McLoud
Groff. See Perrin
Grovenor. See Winslow
Grover. Revolutionary Pension Records: Ebenezer Grover (Conn.), p 14-15; Ichabod Dickinson (Conn.), p 15-17; John Brittain Bowers (Va.), p 18; Edmund Hewitt (Conn. & N. Y.), p 18; John Willis (Va.), p 18-19; Selah Norton (Conn.- Bible record incl.), p 19; Henry Dugan (Pa.), p 19-20; John Rhodes (N. C.), p 20; Richard Rhodes (R. I.), p 20; Christopher Borders (Va.), p 20; Jacob Lobdell (N. Y.), p 21; John Riland (Va.), p 22; James Bray (N. J., N. Y., Pa.), p 22; George House (Va.), p 22; Thomas McClelland (N. C., Pa.), p 22-3; Abel Pettibone (Mass. & Vt.), p 23-4; John Boutelle (Mass.), p 24; John Morrow (Pa.), p 24; Henry Haas (N. J.), p 24 (by Janis H. Miller & Mabel Van Dyke Baer) SUP #2.
Grover. See Cook
Grummon. See Harris
Grumpacker (Crumpacker). (Germany, Pa.) AN 9-3, p 71-2
Grundy. See Ky., Bardstown
Guillen. See de Guillen
Gumaer. See N. Y., Orange Co.
Gundry, Eldon. See Gundry
Gundry, Eldon P. See Drury
Gundry. Gundrys in Virginia (Eldon Gundry) FGQ 4-3, p 42-3
Gunn. See Beardsley; Jaqua
Gunter. See Curtsinger
Gurney. See Staples

(Hemenway, continued) Robert L. Wadland) NE Oct., p 309-10

Henderson-Young (Maine) ML #3, p 44

Henderson. See Adams; Hewitt; N. Y., Hartford

Hendrickson. Who Was Ida, Second Wife of Daniel Hendrickson? (+Van Hengelen, Van Liew, Wyckoff) (by Albert L. Stokes) NJ 37-3, p 111-13

Hendrix, B. S., Jr. See Ala., Tuscaloosa Co.

Hendrix, Roberta Loyster. See Loyster

Henion. See Deyo

Henry. See Houts

Hensley. See Hewitt

Heraldry. The Use of Coats of Arms by Americans (by Lundie W. Barlow) NGS 50-3, p 146-9

Heraldry -- Its Origin & Significance (by Doris Reimann Davidson) GH 16-1, p 28, 31

Herbert, Maybelle. See Welch

Herbert. See Anderson

Herr, Roberta May. See La., Ouachita Parish

Herrington. See Covil

Heselton (1850 Census, Windsor Co., Vt.) AN 9-1, p 19-20

Hewitt. The Identity of Temperance, Second Wife of Jonas Hewitt of Stonington, Conn. (+Holmes, Smith, Treadway) (by Arthur Booth) DS 25-4, p 147-8

Hewitt. Revolutionary Pensions: Joseph Hewitt (Conn.), p 61-2; Jacob Franciscus (Pa.), p 62; James Barnett (Va.), p 62; Andrew House (Va., Pa.), p 63-4; Daniel McClelland (N. C., Pa.), p 64; James Boutell (Conn.), p 64-5; John Dougan (Dungan) (N. C.), p 65; John Cleveland (Conn.), p 65; William Cleaveland (Conn.), p 65-6; Tracy Cleveland (Conn.), p 66; Joseph Henderson (Mass. & N. H.), p 66; Samuel Henderson (Mass. & N. H.), p 66-7; John How (Va.), p 67-8; Jacob Cramer (Md.), p 68; David Royster (Va.), p 69; Thomas

Hewitt, continued) Carpenter (N. Y.), p 70; Samuel Hensley (Va.), p 70-1; John Gay (N. Y.), p 71; Jacob Haas (Pa.), p 71; John Norton (Pa.), p 71; Frederick Cleveland (Conn.), p 71-2; William Taylor (Va.), p 72; Daniel Taylor (N. J.) p 72. SUP #6

Hewitt. See Grover; Howe

Hibbard. See Sanborn

Hicks Bible Record (+Shane) (by Mrs. Jay Ross) SEA 12-1, p191; 12-4, p 221

Hicks. See Barlow

Hickson Bible Record (+Brookes, Miller) (by Noel C. Stevenson) POR 11-10, p 79

Hiday, Nellie C. See Ore.

Higgins. See Franks

High. See Clay

Hildreth, S. P. See Ohio, sources

Hill, Louis C. See Ark., Village

Hill, Mrs. Louis C. See Curtsinger; McLennan; Tex., Falls Co.

Hill. See Bradley; Hanes; Jackson; Jones

Hillborn. See Strickland

Hilling-Corbin (1855 Census, Rensselaer Co., N. Y.) ML #3, p 46

Hillock. See Wilson

Hilton (1855 Census, Delaware Co., N. Y.) ML #1, p 6

Hilton (1855 Census, Delaware Co., N. Y.) ML #2, p 38

Hilts Family Bible Records of Springdale, Ohio (+DuBois, Conover) (by Mrs. Frank L. Baer) HPO 20-4, p 279-80

Hinds. Origin of Rev. Ebenezer Hinds of Bridgewater, Mass. (+Ward, Pratt, Shaw) (by Mrs. John E. Barclay) TAG 38-2, p 70-3

Hinman Bible Record SUP #3, p 27-8

Hinsdale-Manley Samplers NE Oct., p 281-3

Hitchcock. See Glassgow

Hitchings. See Chase

Hite Family (in "Marriages of Some Virginia Residents, 1607-1800") (by Dorothy Ford Wulfeck) VGA, Jan. 19, 1962

(Indiana, continued)

Ind., Tippecanoe Co. Index of Wills, 1845-1864 HG 2-2, p 5-6

Ind., Tippecanoe Co. Durkee Cemetery (Union Twp.) HG 2-2, p 6

Ind., Warren Co. Marriages, 1828-30. (by Mrs. Wilbur T. Leath) HG 2-3, p 6

Ind., Washington Co. Newby Cemetery, Howard Twp. (by Mr. & Mrs. Earl R. Boston) HG 2-3, p 6

Ind., Whitley Co. First Tax Duplicates, 1838 HG 2-5, p 2

Ingalls, Mrs. Robert. See Ind., Lawrence Co.

Ingalls Family Bible Record (+Lamberton, Kellerman) FGQ 4-4, p 69

Ingalls. A Recently Acquired Embroidered Memorial Picture (by Huldah M. Smith) EIH 98-2, p 100-110

Ingalls. See Eveland

Ingham. See Townsend

Ingraham, Duane. See Kans., Trousdale

Ingram. See Millard; "Welcome"

Innes, Alexander. See S. C., Charles Town

Innis. See Lee

Iowa, sources. A Glimpse at Iowa's State Historical Society Library (in Iowa City) (by Mrs. Loren W. Remington) DS 26-2, p 47

Iowa, Cedar Co. (Pennsylvanians mentioned in A History of Cedar Co., Iowa, 1878) LM 3-3, p 5

Iowa, Hardin Co. 1885 Census (+Wagner, Johnson, Harrison) AN 9-1, p 8

Iowa, Pottawattamie Co. 1850 Census (+Snow, Potter, Dewitt, Ballard) AN 9-1, p 18-19

Iowa, Story Co. 1885 Census & 1870 Census (+Harrison, Switzer, Foster, Holdredge, Presnall) (by Mrs. R. J. Wagner) AN 9-1, p 6-8

Ireland, Mrs. David E. See Leonard

Ireland, Mrs. David E. Ancestor Table (No. CIX) TAG 38-1, p 54-5

Irey. See McBride

Irish. See Bronn; R. I., Little Compton; Smith

Irwin. See Campbell; Wood

Islam. See Foreign genealogy

Jackson, Carametta M. See Hull

Jackson, Gladys. See N. Y., Chemung Co.

Jackson, Mrs. Thomas E. See Brundige; Wyatt

Jackson Bible Record (+Hill) SUP #1, p 3

Jackson. The Green Jackson Family Bible Record (+Tucker, Green, Bishop, Bruce, Perry) (by Mrs. Arnold Staubach) VG 6-1, p 39-40

Jackson. See Cary; Dodd; Mo., Saline Co.; Postell; Thorne

Jacobus, Donald Lines. See Adams; Durant; Foreign genealogy; Howd; Methods, general; Parsons; Patten; Sources, publications; Torrey

James, Jessie Alla. See Ga., Oglethorpe

James Note (answer to query) MGX 8-1&2, p 39

James. See Rodrick; Wilson

Jameson, Rea Marrs. See Marrs

Jamieson. See Tayloe

Janes. See Mich., Ingham Co.

Jans. See Kip

Jaqua Bible Record (+Gunn, Bunce, Page) SUP #1, p 3-4

Jaquith Family (by Jessie Palmer Williams) NGS 50-1, p 37-42

Jayne. See Millard

Jefferson. See Marvel

Jenison. Hiram Jenison (1813-1889) MI 8-1, p 5

Jenkins, Nelle Morris. See Ala., Conecuh Co., Marengo Co.

Jenkins. See Hanes

Jenks. See Smith

Jeune. See Dan

Jeuriaens. See Van Doren

Jewett. See Boynton; Edwards

Jinnings. See Webber

Johns. See Moyle

Johnson, C. K. See McPherson

Johnson, Hilda. See Ohio, Clermont Co.

Johnson Coat-of-Arms (with family data) (by Hazel Kraft Eilers) HO 67-1, p 125-7

Johnson-Thomas Bible Record SUP #3, p 31-3

Johnson. See Beavers; Brundige; Chase; Griswold; Iowa, Hardin Co.;

Kuikendal. See N. Y., Orange Co.
Kuykendall, Rhea. See Rider
Kuzmic, Martha. See Marshall; Mo., Saline Co.

Lake. John Lake Family Record (+Matthews) (by Alice D. Serrell) DS 26-2, p 75
Lakin. See Bartholow
Lamb-Garfield (Mass., Vt.) ML #4, p 72-3
Lamb. The Widow Emery Lamb Late of Boston (by Winifred Lovering Holman) NE April, p 152
Lamberton. See Ingalls
Lamoreaux. See Utah, Davis Co.
La Motte. See Hamtramck
Lampes. See Rea
Lamphier, Mrs. Arthur. See Rodman
Lamphier (1850 Census, Herkimer Co., N. Y.) ML #1, p 13, 18
Lamphier. See Bennett
Lampton. See Cason
Lancaster. See Hanson; Ky., Bardstown
Landes, Mrs. H. R. See Landes
Landers, J. P. See Fulgham
Landes. One Branch of the Landes Family (by Mrs. H. R. Landes) TS 4-4, p 90-1
Landry, Louis C., Jr. See La., military records
Lane. See Bearden; Griffin; Hamtramck
Langlos. See Ala., Clarke Co.
Lanning. See Beavers
Lapp, Dorothy B. See Pennsylvania
Larson. See Hult
Lasell (1850 Census, Windsor Co., Vt.) ML #2, p 38
Latta. See Ala., Hale Co.
Laughlin. See Lightcap
Lawrence. See Moyle
Lawton. See Bowdish
Lawyer, Catharine D. See N. Y., Schoharie Co.
Lea Coat-of-Arms (with family data) (by Hazel Kraft Eilers) HO 67-3, p 124-5
Leach, Phyllis. See Blood; Holmes
Leath, Mrs. Wilbur T. See Ind., Warren Co.
LeClaire. See Davis
Leddick, Grace. See N. Y., Saratoga Co.
Ledley, Wilson V. See Bennet; Van Doren
Lee, Harry Herbert. See Mumford
Lee, Ruth Kline. See Millard
Lee-Innis Bible Record (by Noel C. Stevenson) POR 11-6, p 47
Lee. A Brief Sketch of the Life of Edmund R. Lee KCG 2-11, p 3-5; 2-12, p 3-5
Lee. See Fitzsimmons; Millard
Leech, Phyllis. See Ashton; Leach
Leech, Roy. See Pa., Westmoreland Co.
Leeman. See Robinson
Legg. See Francisco
leGrand. See correction note in NYR listing, p 8, GPA INDEX 1962
LeHue, James H. See Mo., Callaway Co.
LeHue, James A. See Mo., Reedsville
LeHue, James. See W. Va., Wetzel Co.
Leland, Isabella Middleton. See Middleton
Lelwards. See Wood
Lemley. See Turnbow
Lemon. Family Bible Record of Robert Lemon, Sr. (of Columbia, Mo.) (+Spence) (by Mrs. William Green Roberds) DAR 96-12, p 744-5
Leonard. Solomon Leonard Descendants, Mayflower Eligibility: Medina County, Ohio, Families (by Mrs. David E. Ireland) OR 3-3, p 125
Leroy. See Vanderburgh
Lewallen. The Lewallen Family Cemetery & Bible Records (Temple, Bell Co., Tex.) (by Raymond H. Bostick OH 3-3, p 75-6; 3-4, p 103-4
Lewis, Mark C. See Yeardley
Lewis. Eleanor Parke Lewis to Mrs. C. C. Pinckney (by Alston Deas) SCH 63-1, p 12-17
Lewis. The Lewis Albums (Ludwig (Lewis)-Klingemann, of Philadelphia, Pa.) (by Oliver E. Allen) beautifully illus. AH 14-1, p 65-80
Lewis. See Franklin; French; Van Vlack

(Maryland, continued)
others) AN 9-5, p 116
Md., Dorchester Co. Tombstone Records (continued from 3-1, p 20) Grace P.E. Church, Taylors Island; Skinner Farm Graveyard and "Arthur's Seat" Farm, Town Point, MDG 3-2, p 42-4: Graveyards on farms "Mitchell Garden" (Mitchell-Moore & others), "Grass Reeden," "Hackett's Adventure" (Hackett graves & others), MDG 3-3, p 62: Graveyards at Old School Meeting on Fishing Creek in Madison Dist., Meekins Neck; Graveyards on farm of Mrs. Wilbur Meekins, Meekins Neck, Hoopers Island Dist. (Meekins & others); Dunnock (& others) Graveyard, MDG 3-4, p 82 (by Nellie M. Marshall)
Md., Frederick Co. See Pennsylvania
Md., Harford Co. Deer Creek Friends Meeting Cemetery (by Janet A. Curtis) SGX 3-23, p 35-6
Md., Kent Co. A List of Early Settlers of Kent Island, 1652 (by Raymond B. Clark, Jr. & Sara Seth Clark) MDG 3-3, p 64
Md., Kent Co. (Notes on Citizens of Kent & Queen Anne's Cos., Md., in) "A Cargo of Flour Presented in 1775 by the Provincial Convention of Md. to the 'Province of Massachusetts Bay'" (a ship) (by L. Wethered Barroll) MHM 57-4, p 371-4
Md., Queen Anne's Co. See Md., Kent Co.
Md., St. Mary's Co. Wills (cont. from 3-1, p 5 (Calvert, Tuttey, Cox, Thomson, Mekarell, Allen (Allin), Payne, Hebden, MDG 3-2, p 31-3; Thomson, Wiseman, Hooper, Johnson, Cooper, Hunt, Manners, Longworth, Dixon, MDG 3-3, p 55-7; Cornish, Brough, Stephenson, MDG 3-4, p 78
Md., St. Mary's Co. Wills (1662-1960) (cont. from 9-10, p 218) Combs to Cooper, 10-1, p 7; Cooper to Cusick, 10-2, p 243-244; Daffin to Donaldson, 10-3, p 252-3; Donovan to Drury, 10-8, p 292; Drury to Edelen, 10-9, p 299; Edelen to Fenwick, 10-12, p 320-1. (Index) CSM, issues as above

(Maryland, continued)
Md., Talbot Co. Marriage Licenses (cont. from 3-1, p 7) (by Raymond B. Clark, Jr. & Sara Seth Clark) MDG 3-2, p 29-30; 3-3, p 54; 3-4, p 77
Md., Talbot Co. Feature: Talbot Co., & Its Tercentenary (Raymond B. Clark, Jr.) MDG 3-4, p 74-5
Md., Talbot Co. A Guide to the Genealogical Records of the Counties of Md. & Del.: Talbot Co. (by Raymond B. Clark, Jr.) MDG 3-4, p 76
Md., Washington Co. Balance Books on Estates, 1778-1782 (by Mrs. P. D. Shingleton) MDG 3-4, p 80
Mason-Riggs (Mass.) ML #1, p 10
Mason. See Franks; Mass., Swansea
Massachusetts. A Short Census of Mass., 1779 (cont. from Vol. 49, p 141) (by William H. Dumont) NGS 50-1, p 26-8
Mass. Harvard Classes of 1751-1755 NE April, p 109-112
Mass., vital records. Persons Who Changed Names in 1845 (in Mass.) OKL 7-2, p 312; 7-3, p 318
Mass., vital records. The Rev. Warren Emerson's Marriage Records (by Warner Dumas) NE Oct., p 255-60
Mass., Amesbury. See Davis
Mass., Beverly. A Parish Is Formed, The Precinct of Salem & Beverly, 1713-1753 (by Robert W. Lovett) EIH 98-3, p 129-153
Mass., Boston. See N. Y., New York
Mass., Paxton. Warnings from Paxton., 1775-1783 (by Winifred Lovering Holman) NE Jan., p 79-80
Mass., Plymouth. Earmarks of Livestock, 1636 AN 9-2, p 30-1
Mass., Swansea. Gravestone Records (all Mason family except two) DAR 96-10, p 660
Mather. See Durant
Mathews. See Lake; Sparkman
Matteson. See Millard
Matthews Bible Record (+Hunsinger, Haegele, Daniel) (by Robert F. Haegele) POR 11-9, p 69. See

(Method, Library Research: continued) Mrs. R. F. Pratt) POR 11-8, p 62

Method, library research. Searching for Ancestors: Family & Institutional Records (by Adelle Bartlett Harper) GM 6-2, p 28-9

Method, library research. Library Research (Mrs. R. F. Pratt) TS 4-2, p 56

Method, library research. Public Records for Research (Adelle Bartlett Harper) GM 6-3, p --

Meydon. See Hudson

Meyer, Mary K. See N. Y., Tompkins Co.

Meyers, E. L. (Roy). See Ore., Clackamas Co.

Michigan. Post Offices in Michigan Territory, 1828. (by Mrs. James D. McGlynn) DS 26-2, p 48

Michigan's First Constitution: Its Loss & Restoration (illus.) (by Paul G. Palmer) MH 3-3, p 121-3

Michigan. An 1805 Michigan Territory List of Persons Owing Taxes DS 26-2, p 76

Michigan, military records. Soldiers of the War of 1812 Who Died in Michigan and War of 1812 Soldiers' Widows Who Died in Michigan (by Alice Turner Miller) MH 4-1, p 9-66

Michigan, sources. Research in Michigan MI 8-4, p 7

Michigan, sources. Unique Materials for Michigan Family Research (by Joseph L. Druse) DS 25-3, p 111-15

Mich., Antrim Co. Marriages, 1863-1866. DS 26-2, p 78-9

Mich., Antrim Co. Antrim County Officers Through 1875 As Shown in Book A DS 26-2, p 79-80

Mich., Barry Co. Inscriptions on Two Barry Co. Gravestones (Dewey & Falk) (by Harold D. Burpee) MH 3-3, p 146

Mich., Burr Oak. Cemetery Records - Burr Oak, 1859-1956 (cont. from 3-2, p 116) (by Geneva Smith) MH 3-3, p 170-76

Mich., Delta Mills. Tombstones from Hillside Cemetery at Delta Mills

(Michigan, continued) FGQ 4-4, p 78-9

Mich., Detroit. Records of the First Presbyterian Church (by Mrs. Kenneth Wheeler & Mrs. Neil M. Romeo) DS 26-1, p 27-32; 26-2, p 65-70

Mich., Detroit. 1812: An Age of Anxiety (from letters in Burton Historical Collection, Detroit Public Library, of Judge James Witherell of Detroit) DS 26-1, p 1-3

Mich., Flint. Earliest Records of St. Paul's Church FGQ 4-4, p 74-5

Mich., Flint. A History of St. Paul's Parish (by Laura Morgan) MH 3-3, p 167-9

Mich., Flint. Inscriptions from Tombstones of Civil War Veterans (Old City Cemetery, now in Avondale Cemetery) (by Merle G. Perry, Jr.) FGQ 4-1, p 4

Mich., Flint. From Record Book of Rev. D. E. Brown (first Pastor of St. Paul's Episcopal Church) FGQ 4-3, p 49

Mich., Genesee Co. Marriage Records of Genesee Co., Mich. (cont. from 3-4) FGQ 4-1, p 6; 4-2, p 40; 4-3, p 58-9; 4-4, p 66-7

Mich., Genesee Co. Genealogical Data Taken from Wills Over 100 Years Old. FGQ 4-1, p 5; 4-2, p 29; 4-3, p 57; 4-4, p 68

Mich., Genesee Co. Original Land Records (Gaines Twp.) (cont. from previous issues) FGQ 4-1, p 18-19; 4-2, p 37-8; 4-4, p 70-72

Mich., Ingham Co. Pioneer Ingham Co. Families (cont. from 3-2, p 110) (+Howell, Coulson, Janes, Judson) (by George L. Hammell) MH 3-3, p 124-6

Mich., Ionia Co. Steel Cemetery, Orange Twp. (by Helen Lee Remington) MI 8-3, p 3-4

Mich., Kalamazoo Co. Historical Markers & Memorials (illus.) (by Alexis A. Praus) MH 3-4, p 201-26

Mich., Kalamazoo Co. First Land

(Millard, continued)
Goff, Hix, Bowen, Wright, Martin, Gilmore, Lovering, Richardson, Foster, Howard, Slocum, Ellis, Pierce, Brown, Angell, Rogers, Morse, Wise, Newell, Draper, Arnold, Whipple, Bicknell, Slack, Stevens, Ballou, Marshall, Aldrich, Carpenter, Sly, Rice, Williams, Amesbury, Cobb, Chase, Dyer, Clopper, Harris, Sturgis, Hailes, Smith, Winslow, Matteson, Nichols, Calef) DS 25-3, p 103-10: (Hancock, Ripley, Carey, Smith, Nicolson, Hayden, Reed, Ingram, Gardner, Davis, Flinn, Ridgway, Holbrook, Morris, Speakman, Wadsworth, Gibbons, Fuller, Taylor, Farrington, Richards, Little, Lee, Holland, Colegrove, Jones) DS 25-4, p 149-156: See also following entry

Millard. Descendants of Robert Millard, 1702-1784, of Rehoboth, Mass. & Pawling, N. Y. (by Ruth Kline Lee) (Eddy, Robinson, Taylor, Burcham, Hull, Hunter) DS 26-1, p 22-6: (Willoughby, Hopkins, Boyce, Strickland, Kingsley, Eaton, Armstrong, Fillmore, Bran, Luby, Akin (Aitken), Scoby, Tripp, Finn, McDaniel, Tingley, Bell, Harding, Jayne, Ashley, Draper, Bartholomew, Andrews) DS 26-2, p 51-4

Millbrook, Minnie Dubbs. See Caywood

Millbrook, Mrs. Raymond. See Wood

Miller, Alice Turner. See Mich., military records

Miller, Janis. See Green

Miller, Janis H. See Grover

Miller. Inscriptions from Miller Graveyard in Craig Co., Va. (near New Bethel Church, 15 mi. north of Newport) (+Peck) AN 9-3, p 60

Miller. See Hall; Hickson; Kieffer

Millet. See Holbrook

Millikan. See Wyatt

Millspaugh. See Clement

Milner-Brooks (Va., Ala.) ML #3, p 51

Milum-Angel (1860 Census, Marion Co., Ark.) ML #5, p 100

Minshall Coat-of-Arms (with family data) (by Hazel Kraft Eilers)

(Minshall, continued)
HO 66-12, p 125-6

Miscellaneous. The Lively Historians MH 3-3, p 134, 154

Miscellaneous. Religion in the Early Colonies REF 4-1, p 4-6

Miscellaneous. Number of White Inhabitants in North America, 1755. JNC 8-3, p 1005-6

Miscellaneous. Dollars and Sense? (by Helen Moulton Meanwell) DS 25-3, p 132-3

Mishey. See Dennis

Mississippi, military records. War of 1812 Pensioners (with Miss. connection) MGX 8-1&2, p 17-20

Mississippi, vital records. Miscellaneous Mississippi Marriages (from 1850 census of Leake, Madison, Attala, Issaguena (none) counties) MGX 8-1&2, p 32-3

Miss., Amite Co. 1850 Census (Parker, Westbrook, Gray) AN 9-6, p 144

Miss., Attala Co. See Miss., vital records

Miss., Franklin Co. 1820 Census MGX 8-1&2, p 24-31

Miss., Grenada Co. Deed Book I (by Mrs. J. W. Martin) MGX 8-1&2, p 5

Miss., Lafayette Co. Sale of Government Lands MGX 8-1&2, p 21-3

Miss., Leake Co. See Miss., vital records

Miss., Madison Co. See Miss., vital records

Miss., Tishomingo Co. Marriages MGX 8-1&2, p 14-16

Miss., Wayne Co. The Gaines Invincibles (1861) MGX 8-1&2, p 31-2

Missouri, military records. Muster-in-roll, Missouri State Militia; Capt. Henry O. Clark, April 29, 1865 (by Mrs. W. F. Van Pelt) POR 12-3, p 22

Missouri, military records. Company F, 50th Missouri Infantry, Civil War POR 12-1, p 5

Mo., Callaway Co. Cemetery Records:

Nelson. See Armfield; Wilson

Nesbitt. War of 1812 Pensions: Nathaniel Nesbitt (Md., Pa.), p 62-3; Jacob Appleton (Pa.), p 72 SUP #6

Nesbitt. War of 1812 Pensions: John Nesbitt (Md.), p 37; Jacob Shilts (Pa.), p 37; James Francisco (Tenn.), p 45; Solomon Main (Pa.), p 46. SUP #4

Nevins, Archie Prentiss. See Nevins

Nevins. The Nevins Family: Descendants of Thomas Nevins, Hollis, N. H. (cont. from 3-2, p 93) (+Newton, Gifford, Wickham, Gurnsey, Coddington, Waxham, Gardener) (by Archie Prentiss Nevins) MH 3-3, p 135-40; 3-4, p 195-9

Newby. See Ind., Washington Co.

Newell. See Chamberlain; Holbrook; Millard; Owen

Newhall Bible Record (+Buxton) (by Noel C. Stevenson) POR 11-9, p 71

New Hampshire, Cheshire Co. Location of Graves of Revolutionary Soldiers: Towns of Westmoreland, Winchester. (cont. from DAR, Dec. 1961) DAR 96-1, p 37-8

N. H., Coös Co. Location of Graves of Revolutionary Soldiers: Towns of Carroll, Clarksville, Colebrook, Columbia, Dalton, Dummer, Errol, Gorham, Groveton, Jefferson, Lancaster, Milan, Northumberland, Pittsburg, Randolph, Shelburne, Stark, Stewartstown, Stratford, Wentworth Location, Whitefield. DAR 96-1, p 37-8

N. H., Grafton Co. Location of Graves of Revolutionary Soldiers: Towns of Alexandria, Ashland, Bath, Benton, Bethlehem, Bridgewater, Bristol, Campton, Canaan, Dorchester, Easton, Enfield, Franconia, Grafton, Groton, Hanover; DAR 96-2, p 161-2: Towns of Haverhill, Hebron, Holderness, Landaff, Lebanon, Lisbon, Littleton, Lyman, Lyme; DAR 96-4, p 388-9: Towns of Munroe, Orange, Orford, Piermont, Plymouth, Rumney, Thornton, Warren, Wentworth, Woodstock; DAR 96-5, p 505-7

N. H., Hillsboro Co. Location of

(New Hampshire, continued)
Graves of Revolutionary Soldiers: Towns of Amherst, Antrim, Bedford, Bennington, Brookline, Deering, Francestown, Goffstown; DAR 96-5, p 505-7: Towns of Greenfield, Hancock, Hillsboro; DAR 96-6, p 548-9: Town of Hollis; DAR 96-8 p 617

New Jersey. Baptist Marriage Records of Rev. Levanus Myers for 1887-1912 (while Pastor of Bethlehem Baptist Church, 1887-8; Pittsgrove Baptist, 1888-91; Daretown Baptist 1891-6; Canton Baptist of Lower Alloways Creek, 1896-1904; Anglesea Baptist of Wildwood, 1911-12. NJG 9-2, p 358-61

New Jersey. Vandalism in Cemeteries Must Be Stopped NJG 9-4, p 377, 379

New Jersey. Rateables, 1773-1774 (cont. from Vol. 36, p 130) (by Charles Carroll Gardner & Kenn Stryker-Rodda) Explanation in 37-3, p 114-5. See also individual townships. NJ 37-1, p 24-32; 37-2, p 71-79; 37-3, p 114-21

N. J., Bound Brook. Presbyterian Church Baptisms (by Dorothy A. Stratford) NJ 37-2, p 65-70

N. J., Cape May Co. Lower Precinct Rateables, July 1773 and July 1774 (in "N.J. Rateables, 1773-4") (by Charles Carroll Gardner & Kenn Stryker-Rodda) NJ 37-3, p 119-21

N. J., Freehold. Records of the Dutch Congregations of Freehold & Middletown (cont. from Vol. 36, p 141) (by Edward J. Raser) See corrections (to 37-2, p 87, 90, 91) in 37-3, p 134.
NJ 37-1, p 41-8; 37-2, p 82-93; 37-3, p 135-44

N. J., Hanover. Hanover Presbyterian Church Marriages by Rev. Aaron Condit (cont. from Vol. 36, p 105) (by Henry W. Pilch) NJ 37-1, p 9-19

N. J., Hunterdon Co. Freeholders, 1741 (Townships of Trenton, Hopewell, Maidenhead, Amwell,

(New York, continued)

from the files of the Cayuga Co. Court House, Auburn, N. Y., 1847 TT 2-1, p 5

N. Y., Cayuga Co. Marriages in Auburn in 1847 (cont. from previous issue) TT 2-2, p 24

N. Y., Cayuga Co. Marriages in Aurelius, 1847 TT 2-2, p 24; 2-3, p 44

N. Y., Cayuga Co. Marriages in Brutus, 1847 TT 2-3, p 44; 2-4, p 68

N. Y., Cayuga Co. Marriages in Cato, 1847 TT 2-4, p 68

N. Y., Cayuga Co. Marriages in Conquest, 1847 TT 2-4, p 68

N. Y., Cayuga Co. See N. Y., Tompkins Co.

N. Y., Chautauqua. Bits of History of Chautauqua (by Mabel Sixby) YY 5-20, p 225-7

N. Y., Chautauqua Co. Harmony (by George C. Fowler) YY 5-19, p 177

N. Y., Chemung Co. The Formation of Chemung Co. and its Towns: A Brief History TT 2-4, p 69

N. Y., Chemung Co. Cemetery Records: Dutch Hill Cemetery (by Gladys Jackson) TT 2-2, p 25; 2-3, p 45

N. Y., Chemung Co. Cemetery Records: Sagetown Cemetery TT 2-4, p 69

N. Y., Chenango Co. Marriages Compiled from "The Chenango Union," a weekly Newspaper published at Norwich, N. Y. (by Mrs. Albert Phillips) TT 2-1, p 6; 2-2, p 26; 2-3, p 46; 2-4, p 70

N. Y., Chenango Co. See N. Y., Oneida Co.

N. Y., Cortland Co. Births in the Town of Freetown, 1847-49 TT 2-1, p 7

N. Y., Cortland Co. Marriages in the Town of Freetown, 1847-48 TT 2-1, p 7; 2-4, p 71

N. Y., Cortland Co. Early Homer (by Bessie B. Butler) illus. YY 5-19, p 162-9

N. Y., Cortland Co. Marriages in Homer, 1847, 1849 TT 2-2, p 27; 2-3, p 47; 2-4, p 71

(New York, continued)

N. Y., Coxsackie. See N. Y., Greene Co.

N. Y., Dutchess Co. Rhinebeck Cemetery (by D. E. Smith) AN 9-5, p 114

N. Y., Genesee Co. The Holland Land Office: The Genesee Story Yesterday & Today (illus.) (by Charllotte M. Read) I. The Land Office Established, YY 6-21, p 27-36; II. The Land Office as a Museum, YY 6-22, p 85-96

N. Y., Genesee Co. See N. Y., Tompkins Co.

N. Y., Greene Co. Marriages of the Dutch Reformed Church of Coxsackie (cont. from Vol. 92, p 244) Oct. 6, 1821 thru 1860, NYR 93-1, p 37-53; 1861 thru 1875, NYR 93-2, p 99-105

N. Y., Hartford. Gravestone Inscriptions in Hartford & Vicinity (cont. from Vol. 115, p 303) (by Isabella Weir Brayton & Florence Ford Fenno): Morningside Cemetery, Hartford, NE Jan., p 57-71: South Hartford Cem.and East Hartford Cem. in Hartford, Townsend Cem. in South Hartford, NE April, p 112-20: West Hartford Cem., Adamsville Cemeteries, Henderson, Briggs, Brayton, Goodell & Sill Cemeteries, NE July, p 205-13

N. Y., Hartland. Birth Records of the Hartland Friends Monthly Meeting (cont. from 5-18, p 120) (by Julia Hull Winner) YY 5-19, p 180-83

N. Y., Hartland. Hartland Friends Records: Removals List, Hartland Monthly Meeting (cont. from 5-19, p 183) (by Julia Hull Winner) YY 5-20, p 242-6; 6-21, p 55-8

N. Y., Jefferson Co. Records (mortality schedules, 1850) (by Ethel B. Swaffer) TT 2-1, p 8; 2-2, p 28; 2-3, p 48; 2-4, p 72

N. Y., Kings Co. Persons Who died During the Year Ending 1 June 1850 (in Gravesend Twp.) (by J. D. Morrell) AN 9-1, p 1-2

(New York, continued)

N. Y., Kings Co. Extracts from "The Brooklyn Eagle & Kings County Democrat."Jan. 19, 1842 AN 9-5, p 99

N. Y., Kings Co. Extracts from "The Brooklyn Daily Eagle" for Sat., Nov. 8, 1851. AN 9-5, p 97-8

N. Y., Lewis Co. Cemetery Records: Collins Cemetery (by Huldah Wendt Hutchins) TT 2-4, p 73

N. Y., Lewis Co. Cemetery Records: Highmarket Protestant Cemetery (by Huldah Wendt Hutchins) TT 2-3, p 49; 2-4, p 73

N. Y., Lewis Co. Old St. Paul's Episcopal Cemetery on West Road, Constableville, N. Y. (by Huldah Wendt Hutchins) TT 2-1, p 9; 2-2, p 29

N. Y., Lewis Co. Thayer Hill Cemetery, Leyden (by Huldah Wendt Hutchins) TT 2-2, p 29

N. Y., Long Island. Long Island's Revolutionary Counterfeiting Plot (by Edward J. Smits) LIH 2-1, p 16-25

N. Y., Madison Co. Guardianship Records, 1806-1878. TT 2-1, p 10; 2-2, p 30; 2-3, p 50; 2-4, p 74

N. Y., Montgomery Co. Subscribers to the First Centenary of Methodism at Palatine Bridge & Canajoharie Methodist Church, 1839 (by Mrs. S. W. Planck, Carol Bussing) TT 2-2, p 31; 2-3, p 51; 2-4, p 75

N. Y., New York. The Reverend Edward Mitchell & His Marriages (by H. Minot Pitman) Baptisms in N. Y. City, 1803-4; Marriages in N. Y. City, 1804-9 and 1812-25; some Boston marriages, 1810-11; a list of Rev. Mitchell's children, NYR 93-3, p 129-38: Marriages in N. Y. City, 1825-34, NYR 93-4, p 226-34

N. Y., New York. Some Materials for Genealogical Research in New York City (by Kenneth Scott) NGS 50-3, p 150-2

N. Y., New York. Records of Trinity Church Parish (cont. from Vol. 92,

(New York, continued)

p 207) Nov. 21, 1794 to Nov. 8, 1795, NYR 93-1, p 22-8; Nov. 8 1795 to July 30, 1797, NYR 93-2, p 75-84; Aug. 2, 1797 to Sept. 15, 1799, NYR 93-3, p 149-57; Sept. 22, 1799 to 1809, NYR 93-4, p 206-21

N. Y., Oneida Co. Protestant Cemetery, Alder Creek (by Huldah Wendt Hutchins) TT 2-2, p 29

N. Y., Oneida Co. Index of Names in Dr. John Foot Trowbridge's Day Book, Bridgewater, 1820-25 TT 2-4, p 76

N. Y., Oneida Co. Cemetery Records: Markers from Brodock Cemetery (by Mrs. Joseph Sanders) TT 2-1, p 11; 2-2, p 32

**N. Y., Oneida Co. 1800 Census of Sangerfield, Chenango (now Oneida) Co. (by Mrs. Albert Phillips) TT 2-3, p 52; 2-4, p 76

N. Y., Onondaga Co. Vital statistics from files of the Onondaga Historical Association TT 2-1, p 12; 2-4, p 77

N. Y., Onondaga Co. Certificates of Conveyances DS 26-2, p 71-4

N. Y., Onondaga Co. Names from Day Book of Dr. Jonas C. Baldwin, 1813-14 (by Pearl Palmer) TT 2-2, p 33; 2-3, p 53

N. Y., Onondaga Co. Birthday Party (of Sarah Adams Coffin, 1887, in Lysander, N. Y.) TT 2-3, p 53

N. Y., Ontario Co. Cemetery Records: Crittenden Cemetery, Phelps Twp.; Oak Lawn Cemetery, Phelps Twp. (by Mrs. Victor E. Pardue) TT 2-1, p 13

N. Y., Ontario Co. Inscriptions from Pinewood Cemetery, Town of Phelps (by Bertha L. McMillan) YY 6-22, p 115-18

N. Y., Ontario Co. South Bristol (by Dorleah K. Simmons) illus. YY 5-19, p 147-50

N. Y., Ontario Co. The Town of Seneca (by Edwin L. Bristol) YY 5-19, p 178-9

N. Y., Orange Co. Peter Gumaer: Early Settler of Deerpark (by

**See also: N. Y., Sangerfield, GPA INDEX, p 61

(New York, continued)
D. Nelson Raynor) (+Codebeck, Davids, Kuikendal, Depuy, Swartwout, VanVliet, Westbrook, Gumaer) illus. YY 6-21, p 16-26

N. Y., Orange Co. The Town of Monroe (by Olive Bull Nozell) illus. YY 6-22, p 71-6

N. Y., Orange Co. Where Is Craigville? A Description of an Industrial Center of Orange Co. (cont. from 5-18, p 90) (by Helen R. Predmore) YY 5-19, p 138-46 illus.

N. Y., Oswego Co. Early Wills Abstracted from Surrogate Records at Oswego Co. Court House TT 2-1, p 14; 2-2, p 34; 2-3, p 54; 2-4, p 78

N. Y., Oswego Co. Marriage Records of Sandy Creek, 1827-68 (by Louise W. Lynch) YY 6-22, p 77-84, 97-100

N. Y., Otsego Co. Exeter Cemetery, Exeter (mainly White Markers, some Clarke, Hubbard, Crandall, etc. markers) (by Mrs. R. E. Long) AN 9-2, p 41; 9-5, p 105-6

N. Y., Petersburg. Earmarks (by Mrs. H. P. Allen) AN 9-1, p 23-4; 9-4, p 76-8

N. Y., Phelps Cemetery in North Part of Town of Phelps (by Bertha L. McMillan) YY 5-19, p 184-5

N. Y., Port Jervis. Archaeological Finds of the Upper Delaware River (by D. Nelson Raynor) illus. YY 5-20, p 221-4

N. Y., Sangerfield. Assessment of Sangerfield, 1796 (by Mabel Woods Smith) TAG 38-3, p 149-51
See also: N. Y., Oneida Co.

N. Y., Saratoga Co. Guardianship Records (by Grace Leddick) TT 2-3, p 55; 2-4, p 79

N. Y., Saratoga. Marriage Notices from Saratoga Sentinel, 1819-37 AN 9-1, p 13-14

N. Y., Saratoga. Saratoga Sentinel Marriage Notices, 1819-1837 AN 9-2, p 31-2

N. Y., Saratoga. "Sentinel" Marriage

(New York, continued)
Notices. AN 9-5, p 101-2

N. Y., Schenectady Co. Marriages in the First Reformed (Dutch) Church of Glenville, 1818-38 (by Donald A. Keefer) TT 2-4, p 80

N. Y., Schoharie Co. Excerpts from the History of Cobleskill by the late Chauncey Rickard (by Norman Olsen) illus. YY 6-21, p 49-54

N. Y., Schoharie Co. Schoharie Co. History in the Gazetteers of the State of N. Y. (by Norman Olsen) illus. YY 6-21, p 45-8

N. Y., Schoharie Co. Town of Fulton (by Catharine D. Lawyer) illus. YY 5-19, p 151-61

N. Y., Schuyler Co. The Underground Railroad: Watkins Glen (by Arthur Richards) illus. YY 5-20, p 214-20

N. Y., Seneca Co. Marriage Records, 1823-38, from First Reformed Dutch Church, Ovid (by Mrs. Cameron F. MacRae III) DS 25-4, p 157-9

N. Y., Seneca Co. Inscriptions from Sheldrake Cemetery, Sheldrake Pt. (+Berlew, Wood) and Evergreen Cemetery, Romulus (+Waugh) AN 9-6, p 135

N. Y., Seneca Co. Sheldrake Cemetery, Sheldrake. (by Mrs. Victor E. Pardue) TT 2-2, p 35; 2-3, p 56; 2-4, p 81

N. Y., Steuben Co. Cemetery Records: Jasper Village Cemetery (by Mrs. Victor E. Pardue & Leora Drake) TT 2-4, p 82

N. Y., Steuben Co. Avoca (by Mary E. Shults) YY 5-19, p 174-6

N. Y., Steuben Co. History of the Town of Caton (by John C. Rose) YY 5-19, p 171-3

N. Y., Steuben Co. "The Old Men of Jasper," Steuben Co., in 1876 (by Leora Wilson Drake) YY 5-19, p 188

N. Y., Tioga Co. Births in 1847 in Town of Berkshire; Births in 1848 in Town of Nichols, TT, 2-3, p 57; Births in 1847 in Town of Owego,

(Ohio, continued)

(Ohio, continued)

Ohio, Morgan Co. Estates & Guardians, 1838-1856 OR 3-1, p 5-6; 3-2, p 69-70

Ohio, Morgan Co. Early County Commissioners OR 3-2, p 70

Ohio, Paulding Co. Vagaries of the Paulding Co. Census Takers, 1850 (by Milton Rubincam) NGS 50-2, p 115-16

Ohio, Perry Co. Shawnee Cemetery OR 3-3, p 118-19

Ohio, Perry Co. See Ohio ("Land Grants..")

Ohio, Portage Co. Court House Records: Wills & Administrations, 1817---. (cont. from previous issues) OR 3-1, p 35-9

Ohio, Portage Co. Deaths of Aged Persons in Nelson.. Reported in the "Garrettsville Journal" (reprinted in the "Western Reserve Chronicle, Jan. 23, 1878, Warren, Ohio) OR 3-3, p 113

Ohio, Richland Co. Cemetery Records of Ohio: Old Salem (Lutheran) Cemetery in Richland Co.: Ross Cemetery in Butler Co. (surname only) OGS 2-5, p 4

Ohio, Richland Co. Pioneer Directory & Scrapbook (list of aged Richland Co. people, 1887) OGS 2-2, p 2; 2-3, p 2; 2-5, p 4

Ohio, Richland Co. Will Index OGS 2-4, p 3

Ohio, Richland Co. Veterans of the War of 1812 OGS 2-4, p 2

Ohio, Richland Co. Court Records: Deeds, 1814-1825 (1826). OR 3-1, p 15-17; 3-2, p 88-91; 3-3, p 143-7; 3-4, p 190-95

Ohio, Richland Co. Cemetery Records: Presbyterian Cemetery (surname only) OGS 2-1, p 3

Ohio, Richland Co. Cemetery Records of Ohio: Adario Cemetery, Church of God Cemetery (surname only) OGS 2-4, p 3

Ohio, Richland Co. Cemetery Records of Ohio: Evangelical German Reform Cemetery (surname only) OGS 2-3, p 3

(Ohio, continued)

Ohio, Richland Co. Cemetery Records: Ganges Cemetery (surname only) OGS 2-2, p 3

Ohio, Sciota Co. Early Marriage Records OR 3-1, p 40-1

Ohio, Sciota Co. Early Deeds OR 3-1, p 41

Ohio, Springfield. Friendship Quilt (by Harvey O. Portz) OR 3-4, p 171

Ohio, Summit Co. Marriage Records (+Darrow, Prior, Wilcox) AN 9-2, p 25

Ohio, Trumbull Co. People in Fowler Township, All Over 70 Years of Age in 1788: "Western Reserve Chronicle, Aug. 22, 1877, Warren, Ohio OR 3-3, p 113

Ohio, Tuscarawas Co. Fiat Cemetery OR 3-1, p 22-5

Ohio, Tuscarawas Co. Roswell Cemetery OR 3-1, p 28

Ohio, Washington Co. See Pierrot

Ohio, Wayne Co. Court House Records: Marriages, 1813-1818, Original Contracts OR 3-3, p 105-109

Ohio, Windsor Cemetery Inscriptions (by D. Sloan) AN 9-5, p 106-107

Okeson. See Thorne

Okla., Ingalls. Ingalls Cemetery Record (cont. from 6-4, p 265) OKL 7-2, p 299-300; 7-3, p 319-321

Okla., Kay Co. 1902 Roster of Government Employees; and Football & Baseball Teams at Chilocco, ca. 1901-2. OKL 7-3, p 317-18

Olds. See Hull

Olentine. See Powers

Olive Notes (Olive Hotchkiss Cartwright) BCT 5-6, p 8

Olmstead Bible Records (+Parks, Reese) (by Genevieve Beall Porter) MH 3-4, p 227-8

Olney. See Smith

Olsen, Norman. See N. Y., Schoharie Co.

Oman. See Swank

Oregon. Early New Jersey Families to Oregon Territory, Taken from the Donation Land Claims of Oregon

(Pennsylvania, continued)
Wills, 1770-1800 (cont. from Dec., 1961) (by Charlotte Hay Beard) DAR 96-2, p 162-3
Penn., Blair Co. Blair County (1788 assessments & notes) YFT 10-3&4, p 100
Penn., Bradford Co. Items (cont. from Vol. 10, #2) (by Margaret E. Rowley & Muriel Link) YFT 10-3&4, p 86-8; 11-1, p 17-18
Penn., Butler Co. Early Settlers (by Brenda Hegner) YFT 10-3&4, p 92-4
Penn., Chester Co. Deaths, 1852-1855 (cont. from Vol. 10, #2) YFT 10-3&4, p 83-5
Penn., Chester Co. See Kansas
Penn., Cumberland Co. See Penn., Bedford Co.
Penn., Dauphin Co. Dauphin County (assessment lists, 1749-50, then Lancaster Co.) YFT 10-3&4, p 96-7
Penn., Franklin Co. Wills, Book B (cont. from Vol. 10, p 42) YFT 10-3&4, p 68-70; 11-1, p 5-6
Penn., Fulton Co. (Cemetery Records of) Wells Valley Methodist Cemetery, Wells Twp.; Wells Valley Evangelical & United Brethern; Bethel Cemetery, Wells Valley. YFT 10-3&4, p 101-103
Penn., Fulton Co. See Penn., Bedford Co.
Penn., Huntingdon Co. Huntingdon County (pioneer families) YFT 10-3&4, p 98-100
Penn., Huntingdon Co. See Penn., Bedford Co.
Penn., Indiana Co. Zion Lutheran Cemetery (by Blaine Helman) YFT 11-1, p 9
Penn., Lancaster Co. See Penn., Dauphin Co.
Penn., Lebanon Co. Taxables of Bethel Township, 1782 YFT 11-1, p 19-20
Penn., Lebanon Co. Moravian Church of Bethel, Bethel Township (burial records & notes) YFT 10-3&4, p 104-5
Penn., Mercer Co. List of Donation Land to Revolutionary Soldiers, Mercer Co., Dist. Four (cont. from Vol. 10, #2) YFT 10-3&4, p 76-8;

(Pennsylvania, continued)
YFT 11-1, p 3-4
Penn., Philadelphia. Records from Christ Church (Episcopal) (by Mrs. W. Eckert) (See correction in AN 9-6, p 122 AN 9-5, p 111
Penn., Philadelphia. Philadelphia's Colonial Poor Laws (by Hannah Benner Roach) PGM 22-3, p 159-69
Penn., Philadelphia. Taxables in Chestnut, Walnut & Lower Delaware Wards, Phila., 1767 PGM 22-3, p 170-85
Penn., Philadelphia Co. Administration Book "C" (11 April 1720-13 June 1737) (by Mrs. Georges Carousso) PGM 22-4, p 238-73
Penn., Somerset Co. From "Pastors and People of Somerset Classic" TS 4-2, p 58-60
Penn., Somerset Co. See Penn., Bedford Co.
Penn., Venango Co. (data from The Franklin Intelligencer of Franklin, 1837-1876) (cont. from Vol. 10, p 46) (by Mrs. William A. Morrison) YFT 11-1, p 14-16
Penn., Washington Co. Marriage Records (cont. from Vol. 10, #2, p 44) YFT 10-3&4, p 89-91; YFT 11-1, p 26
Penn., Westmoreland Co. Deaths (cont. from Vol. 10, p 49) YFT 10-3&4, p 65-7; 11-1, p 7-8
Penn., Westmoreland Co. Presbyterian Church Records, Franklin Twp., 1828-1868 (by Roy Leech) YFT 10-3&4, p 64-5
Penn., Westmoreland Co. Revolutionary Soldiers from Westmoreland Co. (by Brenda Hegner) YFT 11-1, p 25
Pennsylvania. See also: Emigrants; Ill., Warren Co.; Iowa, Cedar Co.
Penoyer. Josephine (Brown) Penoyer (Brown & Penoyer data) (by Mrs. Frank H. Brown) STA 4-8, p 89
Penrose. The Penrose Family of Wheldrake & Ballykean & Their Descendants in Both Hemispheres (by George E. McCracken) NE Oct., p 237-55
Pensions. See Military records

(Texas, sources, continued)
Texas, sources. Early Texas Newspapers (by Marion Day Mullins) STI 2-2, p 48-9
Tex., Atascosito Dist. The 1826 Atascosito District Census (cont. from previous issue) HOU 4-1, p 3-11
Tex., Austin. The Episcopal Church in Austin, Tex. (from a St. David's Church leaflet of 1956) (+Tays, Gregg) AUS 3-2, p 91-2
Tex., Austin Co. Early Austin Co., Texas, families (cont. from Dec. 1961) (+Clemmons, Cleveland, Campbell, Dabney) (by Olive Cartwright) STI 2-1, p 13-15; 2-4, p 131
Tex., Bell Co. See Lewallen
Tex., Bexar Co. Mt. Olive Cemetery Records (between Adkins & Sayers, in Bexar Co.) (by Mrs. A. W. Swinebroad) OH 3-3, p 76-7; 3-4, p 104-6; 4-1, p 12-13
Tex., Bexar Co. Marriage Records (Book A, 1837-1848) (cont. from 2-2, p 44) (by Mrs. R. R. Hunter, Mrs. J. H. Derden, Mrs. Roy Keith) OH 3-2, p 33-4; 3-3, p 63-5; 3-4, p 96-7; 4-1, p 5-7
Tex., Clarksville. The Northern Standard (newspaper) (list of deaths in 1842-1844) (by Marion Day Mullins) STI 2-3, p 95
Tex., Coryell Co. Station Creek Cemetery (near Oglesby) (Mr. & Mrs. Harry L. King) BCT 5-3, p 3-4
Tex., Deaf Smith Co. Marriage Record Book 1 (by Mrs. Lorene Newman, LeRoy Hutton) REF 4-3, p 28-36
Tex., El Copano. See Tex., Rockport
Tex., Falls Co. Early Marriages (1854-61): Marriage Book # 1 (by Mrs. Louis C. Hill) BCT 5-4, p 5-6
Tex., Gonzales Co. Gonzales Co. Records, 1837-1889: Scholastic Census for 1863 taken by J. S. Baldridge OH 3-2, p 37-9; 3-3, p 68; 3-4, p 100-101; 4-1, p 9-10
Tex., Hill Co. Marriage Record Book # 1 (cont. from Nov.-Dec., 1961)
(Texas, continued)
BCT 5-1, p 9-10
Tex., Houston. Vital Statistics from The Telegraph and Texas Register (newspaper) (by Mrs. Guy A. Blount) STI 2-2, p 42-5; 2-3, p 91-3; 2-4, p 119-124
Tex., Indian Gap. Cemetery Inscriptions: Indian Gap, Tex. (by Mrs. A. D. Rooke) OH 3-3, p 73-4
Tex., Indianola. Notes on Indianola, and Cemetery Records (by Mrs. C.N. Fry) OH 4-1, p 18
Tex., Karnes Co. (?) Cemetery Records (between Runge & Kennedy, Tex.) (by Lauretta Russell) OH 3-2, p 43-4
Tex., Lamar. See Tex., Rockport
Tex., McLennan Co. Marriages See listing for BCT in GPA INDEX 1962, p 2
Tex., Nacogdoches. Nacogdoches Under Nine Flags: (1812-1836) (by Lela Whitton Hegarty) OH 3-2, p 39-41; 3-3, p 71-2; 3-4, p 101-3; 4-1, p 10-12
Tex., Nacogdoches. Oak Grove Cemetery Records (by Lela W. Hegarty) OH 3-2, p 41-3; 3-3, p 72-3
Tex., Navarro Co. Persons Born in Alabama (by Mrs. Thomas McMillan George III) ALA 4-1, p 24-6
Tex., Navarro Co. Excerpts from the Navarro Express (1859) (by Suzanne Calhoun George) BCT 5-5, p 10
Tex., Navarro Co. Names from Early Court Records of Navarro Co. (by Mrs. T. M. George III) BCT 5-3, p 5-6; 5-4, p 3-4
Tex., Navarro Co. Marriage Records, Book A, 1846-1857 (by Suzanne Calhoun George) OH 3-3, p 66-7; 3-4, p 99-100; 4-1, p 7-8
Tex., Polk Co. Livingston Cemetery (by Cecyle & Tom Kinard) STI 2-2, p 51-5
Tex., Potter Co. Potter County's State Representatives REF 4-1, p 3
Tex., Potter Co. Marriage Records (Books 1 & 2, to March 14, 1906) (cont. from Oct., 1961) (see also

(Van Doren, continued)
Van Doren. Some Van Doren Records (by R. W. Evans) NJG 9-4, p 384
Van Doren. See Bodine
Van Dusen. See Drury
Van Eaton Family Bible Record (+Young, Stapleton, Bigger) (by Mrs. Anson Blaker) SEA 11-8, p 162; 11-9, p 171
Van Eyderstyne. See Hotchkiss
Vangies. See Forshee
Van Hengelen. See Hendrickson
Van Horn. See Van Buskirk; Wyatt
Van Horne. See Howe
Van Kouwenhoven. See correction notice in NYR listing, GPA INDEX 1962, p 8
Vanlandingham. See Sparkman
Van Lieu-Stout Bible Record SUP #5, p 52-3
Van Liew. See Hendrickson
Van Middlesworth. See Franklin
Vann. See Rogers
Van Natter. See Howe
Van Pelt, Mrs. W. F. See Mo., Civil War
Van Pelt. See Bennet; Wing
Van Siekle. See Pease
Van Slake. See Vrooman
Van Urk, Wilma. See Kip
Van Vlack Bible Record (+Lewis) (by Noel C. Stevenson) POR 12-4, p 31
Van Vleck. See Kip
VanVliet. See N. Y., Orange Co.; Vliet
Van Wagener, Isabella. See Truth
Van Wyck. See Thorne
Vassar, James O. See Va., vital rec.
Vaughan. See Allen
Vaughn-McDaniel (Va., Ky.) AN 9-4, p 84-5
Vaughn. See Bootes; Ga., Twiggs Co.
Veach. See Allen
Verbrycke. See Stoothoff
Verdier. See Winter
Vt., Burlington. Some Burlington, Vt., Marriage Records, 1844 (by Marie Dickore & Ruth Means) NE July, p 186-7
Vt., Franklin Co. Cemetery Inscriptions (Fairfield Pond Road, Fairfield) (by Mrs. J. W. Boyesen)

(Vermont, continued)
AN 9-2, p 34-7
Vt., Windham Co. Gravestones in Westminster West (+Braley, Ide, Perry) (by D. C. Knoff) AN 9-1, p 5-6
Vt., Windham Co. Index to 1830 Census of Windham Co., Vt. (cont. from 11-3, p 114) SEA 12-1, p 194-5
Verran. See Young
Verser. See Borum
Vincent, Joseph E. See Matthews
Vineyard, Arva Lee. See Mo., Johnson Co., Newton Co.
Virginia. British Mercantile Claims, 1775-1803. VG 6-4, p 147-56
Virginia Women of the Revolutionary Decade, 1774-1784 (by Ann Waller Reddy & Nancy Ferguson) VGA, Jan.5; Jan. 26; Feb. 2; March 9; July 20; July 27; Aug. 8; Dec. 14, 1962
Virginia, military records. Militia & Frontier Defense Papers, 1793-1794 VG 6-3, p 132-3
Virginia, sources. Local Notices from the Virginia Gazette, 1780 VG 6-1, p 23-7 (cont. from previous issues)
Virginia, sources. (Genealogical Source Materials & Family Papers acquired by the Virginia Historical Society, 1961) VA 70-2, p 231-2
Virginia, vital records. Some Natives of Virginia Buried in Alabama: Lawrence, Morgan & Colbert Cos. (by James O. Vassar) VG 6-4, p 170-3
Va., Amelia Co. Petition of Amelia Co. Baptists, 27 Oct. 1768. VG 6-2, p 74
Va., Amherst Co. 1800 Tax List. VG 6-1, p 18-22 (cont. from previous issue)
Va., Augusta Co. 1800 Tax List. VG 6-2, p 75-80; 6-3, p 113-20; 6-4, p 157-63
Va., Berkley Co. See Pennsylvania
Va., Brooke Co. See W. Va., Brooke Co.
Va., Brunswick Co. A Guide to the

Washington. See Mo., Reedsville
Washington (State). Pioneer Dead of 1915 SEA 11-9, p 170; 12-1, p 192-3; 12-3, p 210; 12-4, p 219-220
Washington (State). Pioneer Dead of 1911 SEA 11-6, p 144; 11-7, p 149-50; 11-9, p 169-70
Washington (State). Pioneer Data (Pioneers of Washington State) (by Mrs. Wayne W. Prickett) SEA 11-6, p 143-4
Wash., Adams Co. Washington Territory Auditor's Census, Adams Co., 1885 (pages 1-4) Included as supplement to 1962 issues of Bulletin of the Seattle Genealogical Society
Wash., Asotin Co. Washington Territory Auditor's Census, 1885 (pages 11 to 36) Included as supplement with 1962 issues of the Bulletin of the Seattle Genealogical Society
Wash., Chehalis Co. 1871 Census (pages 1 to 4) Included as supplement to 1962 issues of the Bulletin of the Seattle Genealogical Society
Wash., Kitsap Co. Cemetery Records of Port Gamble. SEA 11-7, p 151-2; 11-8, p 164; 11-9, p 171-2
Wash., Kitsap Co. Inscriptions from the Tombstones in the Bethel Cemetery (cont. from 11-3, p 119) SEA 11-5, p 135-6; 11-6, p 142
Wash., Olympia. Bush Prairie (or Pariare) Cemetery (by J. E. Bauserman) AN 9-6, p 126-7
Wash., Olympia. Inscriptions from Bush Pariare Cemetery (by J. E. Bauserman) AN 9-5, p 108-110
Waterhouse Family Bible - Pulaski Co., Ind. (+Ward) (by Mr. & Mrs. John O. Knarr) HG 2-6, p 4
Waterman. See Smith
Watkins-Banning Bible Record (by Noel C. Stevenson) POR 12-1, p 7
Watrous-Tuttle Bible Records (+Marvin) NE Oct., p 286-8
Watson. See Drury; Shannon
Watts. See Hodges
Waugh (1850 Census, Switzerland Co., Ind.) AN 9-4, p 95
Waugh. See N. Y., Seneca Co.
Waxham. See Nevins
Weaner, Arthur. See Loyster
Webb. See Brown; Nichols; Texas
Webber-Jinnings-Harrington (1850 Census, Anderson Co., Tenn.) ML #1, p 20
Weber, Henry. See Ellsworth; Parker
Webster, Olive. See Myrick
Webster. See McLoud; Nevins
Wedge. See Swan
Weeks. See Sparkman
Weinantz, Mrs. Russell. See Ind., Shelby Co.
Weir. See Chatham
Weisert, John J. See Browne
Welch, Edwin C. See Durbin; Welsh
Welch: Surry Co., N. C. Marriages (by Maybelle Herbert) AN 9-1, p 9
"Welcome" (ship) Welcome Notes: A. Jane Bachelour or Batchelor; B. John & Elizabeth (Songhurst) Barber; C. The Buckmans of Billingshurst, Sussex; D. John Ottey's Masquerade; E. The Three Rowlands of Billingshurst; F. Ingram-Thompson-Short; G. Several William Smiths (by George E. McCracken) TAG 38-3, p 152-63
Weldon Bible Record SUP #3, p 31
Weller. See Pritchard
Wellington-Wood-Cogswell Bible Record (by Mrs. Merie Taylor) MH 3-4, p 228
Welsch, Mrs. G. A. See Tex., Travis Co.
Welsh Family Records (+Cannon, Cole, Pogue, Brush) (by Edwin C. Welch) OR 3-2, p 60-63
Welsh. See Ky., Jefferson Co.
Wendell. See Holmes
Wesson (Townsend, Mass., births) AN 9-5, p 99-100
West Family Bible (+Coulson) (by Genevieve Churchill Harris) POR 12-4, p 28
West Family Bible Records: Carroll Co., Ind. (+Willison) (by Mrs. Eugene Bock) HG 2-4, p 6
Westbrook. See Miss., Amite Co.;

(Westbrook, continued)
N. Y., Orange Co.
West Va., Brooke Co. A Guide to the Counties of Virginia (Brooke Co., West Va.) VG 6-1, p 32-4
West Va., Brooke Co. Inscriptions from Lower Buffalo Graveyard, Brooke Co. (by K. T. H. McFarland, III) VG 6-2, p 51-9
West Va., Cabell Co. A Guide to the Counties of Virginia: Cabell Co., W. Va. VG 6-3, p 124-6
West Va., Calhoun Co. A Guide to the Counties of Virginia: Calhoun Co., W. Va. VG 6-4, p 174-5
West Va., Jefferson Co. Melvin Graveyard (at Dust Crossing) JC Vol. 28, p 41-2
West Va., Jefferson Co. Methodist Graveyard, Shepherdstown. JC Vol. 28, p 42-6
West Va., Jefferson Co. Moler Graveyard (on Rose farm along Harpers Ferry Pike) (four other graves also) JC Vol. 28, p 48
West Va., Jefferson Co. Moler Graveyard (near Moler's Cross Roads) (two other graves also) JC Vol. 28, p 47
West Va., Jefferson Co. Moler Graveyard (on Thompson farm near Bakerton) JC Vol. 28, p 49
West Va., Jefferson Co. Moore-Duke Graveyard (on Dittmyer farm along Peachers Mill Road) JC Vol. 28, p 49
West Va., Jefferson Co. Moore Graveyard (near Bardane) JC Vol. 28, p 49-50
West Va., Jefferson Co. "Mount Hammond" Graveyard (1 grave only, Margret H. Little, 1841-2) JC Vol. 28, p 50
West Va., Jefferson Co. Presbyterian Graveyard, Shepherdstown JC Vol. 28, p 52-9
West Va., Jefferson Co. Presbyterian Graveyard (Charles Town) JC Vol. 28, p 50-52
West Va., Wetzel Co. Old Wayman Cemetery Records (by James LeHue) KCG 2-14, p 2
West Va., Wetzel Co. Cemetery Records,

(West Virginia, continued)
Proctor, W. Va. (by James A. LeHue) KCG 2-12, p 5
Wetmore, Psyche Winthrop. See Winthrop
Wetsel. See Smith
Wettenhall. See Hamilton
Whaley (N. Y.) AN 9-4, p 86
Whaley-Hollister (N. Y.) ML #5, p 84
Wheeler, Mrs. Kenneth. See Mich., Detroit
Wheeler. See Dan
Whipple. See Metcalf; Millard; Smith
White. See Chamberlain; Hudson; Methods ("Genealogical Problems" by Moriarty); N. Y., Otsego Co.
Whyte, Donald. See Foreign genealogy; Houston
Whyte Bible Record (+Murray, Cook) (by Noel C. Stevenson) POR 12-1, p 7
Wick Bible Records (+Brown, Eaton) (by Mrs. R. C. Anderson) POR 11-9, p 68
Wickham. See Nevins
Wierman. See Holmes
Wiest. Elizabeth Elmendorf Wiest, Oakland Co. Pioneer (Mich.) (by Marian Leonard Synder) DS 25-3, p 93-5
Wieting (1855 Census, Montgomery Co., N. Y.) ML #4, p 76
Wieting. See Sander
Wiggins. See Franks
Wight-Fanning (Mass., Conn.) ML #3, p 49-50
Wightman. See Bootes
Wilbern, Henry. See Ore., Clackamas Co.
Wilbor. See R. I., Little Compton
Wilbour, Benjamin Franklin. See Case; R. I., Little Compton
Wilbur. See Case; Wood
Wilcockson. See Griffin
Wilcox-Harris (1850 Census, Rock Island Co., Ill.) ML #5, p 98
Wilcox. See Adams; Forsyth; Methods ("Genealogical Problems" by Moriarty); Ohio, Summit Co.; Wyatt

Addenda

BOOKS REVIEWED IN 1962

Book reviews in genealogical periodicals and books of genealogical interest reviewed in other publications

Abilene, Texas, Early Cemetery Records of. 1961. Reviewed in STI 2-4, p 134

Aberdeen, Miss., Bon Accord Historical & Program Booklet for the 125th Anniversary Celebration of. Reviewed in VGA Aug. 10, 1962.

Amy, Henry J. Descendants of David and Amyes (Colle) Thomson, and their son John. 1962. Reviewed in NYR 93-3, p 185-6

Baer, Mabel Van Dyke. "The Ancestry of Edward West of Lexington, Ky., 1757-1827" in The Register of the Kentucky Historical Society, Old State House, Frankfort, Ky. Vol. 58, No. 4, Oct. 1960, pp. 354-366. Reviewed in NGS 50-1, p 46

Bailey, Rosalie Fellows. New England Heritage of Rousmaniere, Ayer, Farwell and Bourne Families. 1960. Reviewed in NGS 50-3, p 165-6; NYR 93-1, p 57-8; TAG 38-2, p 114.

Ball, Bonnie S., James Elihu Ball and Estella Ball Brady. The Balls of Fairfax and Stafford in Virginia. Reviewed in VGA July 27, 1962

Ball, Walter V. The Butterworth Family of Maryland and Virginia...Including Allied Families of Bond, Clark, Clement, Gilbert, Webster, Wheeler and Many Others. 1960. Reviewed in VG 6-2, p 85

Barekman, June B. The Barrackman-Barkman-Barekman Family of Knox Co., Indiana and The Barrackman-Barrickman Families of West Virginia. 1961-1962. Reviewed in STI 2-4, p 133

Batte, R. Bolling. Index to Old Homes and Families in Nottoway, by W. R. Turner. 1961. Reviewed in VG 6-1, p 42.

Beall, William Ryland. Index and Guide to Harper's Weekly and Frank Leslie's Illustrated Newspaper for the Year 1861. Reviewed in VG 6-3, p 139-140

Bell, Raymond Martin. Early Townships in Greene County, Penn. 1961. Reviewed in VG 6-1, p 43

Bell, Raymond Martin. The Ensminger Family. Pennsylvania, Maryland, Virginia, South Carolina. 1961. Reviewed in VG 6-2, p 87-8

Bell, Raymond Martin. List of Inhabitants in Washington County, Penn., 1800 or Before, with Maps of Early Townships, 1776-80 Petition, 1800 County Census. 1961. Reviewed in NGS 50-1, p 45; VG 6-1 p 43

Bell, Raymond Martin. The Seibert Family: Wolfersweiler, Saar; Tulpehocken, Pa.; Clear Spring, Md.; Martinsburg, W. Va. 1959. Reviewed in VG 6-2, p 87-8

Bland Co. (Va.) Centennial Corporation. History of Bland County. 1961. Reviewed in VA 70-3, p 373-4

Blythe, LeGette, and Charles R. Brockmann. Hornet's Nest: The Story of Charlotte & Mecklenburg Co. Reviewed in NCR 39-3, p 379-80

Bonner, Kathryn Rose. St. Francis Co., Ark. Census of 1850. 1962. Reviewed in STI 2-2, p 68; VGA 15 June 1962.

Boone Family Research Association of Missouri, Bulletin of the. 1962. Reviewed in VGA 21 Dec. 1962.

Bordley, James, Jr. The Hollyday & Related Families of the Eastern Shore of Maryland. 1962. Reviewed in NYR 93-4, p 250-1.

Boyd, Hazel Mason, Emma Jane Walker, and Virginia Wilson. Some Marriages of Montgomery Co., Ky., Before 1864. 1961. Reviewed in NGS 50-1, p 45

Boyd, Montague Laffitte, Jr. Genealogical Data: Broyles, Laffitte and Boyd Families. 1959. Reviewed in NGS 50-1, p 45

Bridges, Louise Thonssen. Flags of Louisiana. 1961. Reviewed in LA 9-2, p 26

Brockman, W. E. Genealogical Chart of the Brockmans. 1962. Reviewed in VGA 28 Sept. 1962

Brown, Joseph Parsons. The Commonwealth of Onslow: A History. 1960. Reviewed in NCR 39-1, p 90-91

Bull, Henry de Saussure. The Family of Stephen Bull, 1600-1960. 1961. Reviewed in SCH 63-4, p 241-2

Burns, Annie Walker. Dr. Thomas Walker Family Records, Vol. 1. 1950. Reviewed in VGA 18 May 1962

Bussy, Ethel H. History and Stories of Margaretville and Surrounding Area. 1961. Reviewed in NYR 93-2, p 119

Butt, Marshall W. Portsmouth Under Four Flags, 1752-1961. 1961. Reviewed in VA 70-3, p 358-9

Butterfield, L. H. (ed.) The Adams Papers. 1961. Reviewed in STI 2-1, p 37; STI 2-3, p 110-11

Callahan, North. Daniel Morgan: Ranger of the Revolution. Reviewed in NYR 93-4, p 251-2

Cappon, Lester J. American Genealogical Periodicals: A Bibliography with a Chronological Finding-List. 1962. Reviewed in DS 25-4, p 176; IDA 5-1, p 15; RK 60-3, p 245; TAG 38-4, p 248-9; VA 70-4, p 503-4; VG 6-3, p 136

Chenault, Louise Ryan, John P. and Dorothy Heironimus, and George P. Unseld. The Hieronymus Story. 1959. Reviewed in VG 6-1, p 44

Cline, Mrs. Frank. An Index to the House of Fowler. Reviewed in VGA 2 Nov. 1962

Cook, Gerald Wilson. The Descendants of Claiborne Howard, Soldier of the American Revolution. 1960. Reviewed in NYR 93-2, p 123

Cope, Robert F., and Manly Wade. The County of Gaston: Two Centuries of a N. C. County. 1961. Reviewed in NCR 39-1, p 89-90

Crick, B. R., and Miriam Alman. A Guide to Manuscripts Relating to America in Great Britain and Ireland. 1961. Reviewed in WM 19-2, p 309-11

Daniels, Jonathan. The Devil's Backbone: The Story of the Natchez Trace. Reviewed in NCR 39-4, p 566-7

Davis, Walter Goodwin. The Ancestry of Sarah Johnson, 1775-1824, wife of Joseph Neal of Litchfield, Maine. 1960. Reviewed in NYR 93-1, p 59

Dawson, Aurelia Cate. Our East Tennessee Kindred. Cate, Henry and Related Families. 1962. Reviewed in VG 6-3, p 138-9

des Cognets, Anna Russell, Gov. Garrard of Kentucky, His Descendants and Relatives, and A Postscript About the Garrard Family, by Louis des Cognets, Jr. 1962. Reviewed in FC 36-3, p 285-6; KG 4-4, p 157; SEA 12-2, p 200; SGX 3-24, p 3; TS 4-4, p 88; VG 6-3, p 136-7

de Valinger, Leon, Jr. Court Records of Kent Co., Del., 1680-1705. 1959. Reviewed in WM 19-2, p 319

de Valinger, Leon, Jr., and Virginia E. Shaw. A Calendar of Ridgely Family Letters, 1742-1899, in the Delaware State Archives. 1961. Reviewed in MDG 3-3, p 70

DeVille, Winston. Calendar of Louisiana Colonial Documents: Vol. I (Avoyelles Parish). 1961. Reviewed in La 9-4, p 54

DeVille, Winston. Marriage Contracts of Natchitoches, 1739-1803. 1961. Reviewed in LA 9-3, p 40

DeVille, Winston. Marriage Contracts of Pointe Coupee Post, 1736-1803 (Vol. III): Marriage Contracts of Avoyelles Post, 1792-1800 (Vol. IV). 1962. Reviewed in LA 9-2, p 26

Dickore, Marie. Census for Cincinnati, Ohio, 1817, and Hamilton Co., Ohio,

Votors' Lists, 1798 and 1799. 1960. Reviewed in NGS 50-1, p 45

Dixon, Ben F., and Alice L. (Dwelle) Dixon. Five Generations of American Dwelles. A Family History for Descendants of Lemuel Dwelle and Lavina Francisco, Pioneers of New York and Michigan. Reviewed in NGS 50-1, p 43-4

Doane, Gilbert H. Searching for Your Ancestors. Reviewed in NYR 93-4, p 251

Doherty, Herbert J., Jr. Richard Keith Call: Southern Unionist. 1961. Reviewed in NCR 39-3, p 395-6

Douthit, Ruth Long. Ohio Resources for Genealogists. 1961. Reviewed in NGS 50-3, p 164-5

Douthit, Ruth Long. Some References for Genealogical Searching in Ohio. 1960. Reviewed in NGS 50-3, p 164-5

Dunaway, Jane E. Dunaway-Allder-Pyle Family. 1959. Reviewed in VG 6-1, p 42

Duncombe, Frances R. Katonah: The History of a New York Village and Its People. 1961. Reviewed in NYR 93-4, p 252

Durye, Pierre. La Genealogie. 1961. Reviewed in NGS 50-3, p 162-3

Duvall, Lindsay O. Prince George County...Land Patents, 1666-1719. Virginia Colonial Abstracts, Series 2, Vol. 6. 1962. Reviewed in VG 6-4, p 182

Easterby, J. H., and Ruth S. Green. The Colonial Records of South Carolina, Series 1. Journal of the Commons House of Assembly, Jan. 19, 1748-June 29, 1748. 1961. Reviewed in NCR 39-1, p 95-6; NCR 39-4, p 559; SCH 63-3, p 185

Ellis, Elwood O. Early Friends in Grant Co., Indiana (1825-1913). Reviewed in TAG 38-3, p 192

Everton, George B., Sr. (ed.) The Genealogical Helper. Reviewed in STI 2-4, p 133-4

Everton, George B., Sr., and Gunnar Rasmuson. The Handy Book for Genealogists. 1962. Reviewed in STI 2-2, p 67; VGA 29 June 1962

Fleet, Beverly. Virginia Colonial Abstracts. 1961. Reviewed in VG 6-2, p 84-5

Franklyn, Julian. Shield and Crest: An Account of the Art and Science of Heraldry. 1960, 1961. Reviewed in NE Oct., p 290-92

Frick, George Frederick, and Raymond Phineas Stearns. Mark Catesby, the Colonial Audubon. 1961. Reviewed in SCH 63-1, p 56-7

Frizzell, Martha McD. Second History of Charlestown, N. H., the Old Number Four. 1955. Reviewed in NYR 93-2, p 122

Gee, Mrs. O. K., Sr. History of Middleton, Carroll Co., Miss. 1961. Reviewed in VGA 20 July 1962

Greene, Edward B. Henry Green, Ancestors, Descendants, and Related Families. Reviewed in DS 26-2, p 86

Gregorie, Anne King. Christ Church, 1706-1959, A Plantation Parish of the South Carolina Establishment. 1961. Reviewed in SCH 63-2, p 115

Grimes, Jay Cook. Grimes, Cook and Related Families of Wayne Co., Tenn., A Genealogy. Related Families: Johnson, Morris, Montague, 1800-1960. Reviewed in KG 4-2, p 77

Gwynn, Zoe Hargett. Abstracts of the Records of Onslow Co., N. C., 1734-1850. 1961. Reviewed in NCR 39-1, p 91-2

Gwynn, Zoe Hargett. The 1850 Census of Craven Co., N. C. 1961. Reviewed in NCR 39-1, p 92

Haines, John Wesley. Richard Haines and His Descendants. A Quaker Family of Burlington Co., N. J. Since 1682. 1961. Reviewed in MDG 3-2, p 48

Hale, Richard W. Guide to Photocopied Historical Materials in the United States and Canada. 1961. Reviewed in MDG 3-3, p 70; NCR 39-2, p 247-8; WM 19-4, p 636

Hamer, Philip M. (ed.) A Guide to Archives & Manuscripts in the U. S.: Compiled for the National Historical Publications Commission. 1961. Reviewed in WM 19-2, p 306-7

Harlan, Elizabeth Taft, Minnie Dubbs Millbrook, and Elizabeth Case Erwin. 1830 Federal Census: Territory of Michigan. 1961. Reviewed in NGS 50-3, p 167; TAG 38-2, p 114

Harris, Charles H. The Harris History: A Collection of Histories of Pioneers of Southern Ohio. Reviewed in OR 3-1, p 2

Hasbrouck, Kenneth E. The Hasbrouck Family in America, with European Background. 1961. Reviewed in NYR 93-2, p 120

Hawkins, Nora. Treadway and Buffington Families. Reviewed in SGX 3-24, p 5

Hawks, Francis Lister. History of North Carolina. Reprinted 1961. Reviewed in NCR 39-2, p 220-1

Heiss, Willard C. Guide to Research in Quaker Records in the Midwest. 1962. Reviewed in DS 26-2, p 86; NE Oct., p 293

Heiss, Willard. Honey Creek Monthly Meeting of Friends, Vigo County, Indiana, 1820. Reviewed in TAG 38-3, p 192

Heiss, Willard. A List of All the Friends Meetings That Exist or Ever Have Existed in Indiana, 1807-1955. 1961. Reviewed in TAG 38-1, p 62.

Hemphill, William Edwin, and Wylma Ann Wates. Extracts from the Journals of the Provincial Congresses of South Carolina, 1775-1776. 1960. Reviewed in SCH 63-1, p 55-6

Hickerson, Thomas Felix. Echoes of Happy Valley. 1962. Reviewed in NCR 39-3, p 378

Higginbotham, Don. Daniel Morgan: Revolutionary Rifleman. 1961. Reviewed in SCH 63-2, p 118-19; NCR 39-4, p 576-7

Hill, Harry W. Maryland's Silver Service. 1962. Reviewed in MDG 3-4, p 85

Holcomb-Miller, Cora. History of the Family of Tallon (Talon) in America and Related Families. 1961. Reviewed in STI 2-2, p 68

Hoosier Genealogist, The. 1961. Reviewed in NGS 50-1, p 44

Hopstetter, Mrs. Charles A. Supplement to Illinois Ancestral Directory: Members and Ancestors, DAR. 1962. Reviewed in VGA 23 Nov. 1962

Howe, Daniel Dunbar. Listen to the Mockingbird: The Life and Times of a Pioneer Virginia Family. 1961. Reviewed in VG 6-2, p 86-7

Hutchins, Marvin Clayton. Our Ancestral Heritage: The Ancestors and Descendants of Cicero Mordecai Hutchins and His Wife Frances Carter Sawyer, including Six Generations of Nicholas and Elizabeth (Farr) Hutchins. 1961. Reviewed in TAG 38-2, p 115

Hutchinson, William T., and William M. E. Rachal. The Papers of James Madison. 1962. Reviewed in STI 2-4, p 134

Jenkins, Nelle Morris. Pioneer Families of Sumter Co., Ala. Reviewed in ALA 4-1, p 44

Jennings, Nancy Moores Watts. Texarkana Pioneer Family Histories. 1961. Reviewed in STI 2-1, p 37

Jewell, Mrs. Walter Towner. Loudoun Co., Va., Marriage Bonds, 1762-1850. 1962. Reviewed in VG 6-4, p 180

Johnson, Charles Owen. The Genealogy of Several Allied Families (Owen, Frazer, Bessellieu, Cheche, Johnson, Tidwell, Neill, Briggs). 1961. Reviewed in NYR 93-2, p 123-4

Johnson, William Perry (ed.). The North Carolinian: A Quarterly Journal of Genealogy and History. Reviewed in NYR 93-2, p 121

Johnston, Henry Pollenitz. Little Acorns from the Mighty Oak. Reviewed in ALA 4-1, p 44

Jones, H. G. North Carolina Newspapers on Microfilm. 1962. Reviewed in NCR vol. 39

Julien, Carl, and Daniel W. Hollis. Look to the Rock: One Hundred Ante-bellum Presbyterian Churches of the South. 1961. Reviewed in SCH 63-1, p 58

Keator, Alfred Decker. Keator Family in America: Addenda Et Corrigenda. Reviewed in TAG 38-3, p 192; NGS 50-3, p 166; NYR 93-3, p 187

Kegley, F. B. Kegley's Virginia Frontier, the Beginning of the Southwest, the Roanoke of Colonial Days, 1740-1783. 1962. Reviewed in VG 6-4, p 180

Kellogg, Lucy Mary. A Guide to Ancestral Trails in Michigan. 1961. Reviewed in NGS 50-3, p 167; TAG 38-2, p 114

Kibler, Alta H., Kathy Mancell Cornwell, and Glenn C. Cornwell. The Cornwell-Coulter Chronicle, Part One, Nov. 1961. 1961. Reviewed in VGA 23 Mar. 1962

King, George Harrison Sanford. The Register of Overwharton Parish, Stafford County, Va., 1723-1758, and Sundry Historical and Genealogical Notes. 1961. Reviewed in KG 4-1, p 37; NGS 50-2, p 110-11; VA 70-3, p 356-7; VG 6-2, p 83

Kingsbury, Arthur Murray. Kingsbury Genealogy. 1962. Reviewed in STI 2-2,p 66

Lancaster, Clay. New York's First Suburb: Old Brooklyn Heights, including detailed Analyses of 619 Century-Old Houses. 1961. Reviewed in NYR 93-3, p 187-8

Lawrence, Alexander A. A Present for Mr. Lincoln, the Story of Savannah from Secession to Sherman. 1961. Reviewed in SCH 63-3, p 188

Layne, F. B. Layne-Lain-Lane Family. Reviewed in SGX 3-24, p 3-4

Ledley, Wilson V. New Netherland Families: Van Dien, Van Duyn, and Verduyn. 1960. Reviewed in NYR 93-2, p 121-2

Lee, Rebecca Smith. Mary Austin Holley: A Biography. 1962. Reviewed in STI 2-4, p 135

Leyburn, James G. The Scotch-Irish: A Social History. 1962. Reviewed in MHM 57-4, p 378-9; NCR 39-4, p 567-8; VA 70-4, p 492-3

Lippincott, Ruth B. The Balderston Family. Colora Branch. A Short History of Lloyd and Catharine Canby Balderston of Colora, Md., and Their Children told by Their Children and Grandchildren with some Genealogical Records. 1959. Reviewed in NGS 50-3, p 166-7

Loughlin, Ledlie I. Joseph Ledlie and William Moody; Early Pittsburgh Residents, their background and some of their descendants. 1961. Reviewed in PGM 22-4, p 279-81

McAllister, James A., Jr. Abstracts from the Land Records of Dorchester County, Md. Vol. 4 (Liber Old No. 6) c 1961. Reviewed in MDG 3-2, p 48

McClung, Quantrille D. Carson-Bent-Boggs Genealogy. 1962. Reviewed in CG 23-3, p 80

McCracken, George E. The Penrose Family of Wheldrake, Yorkshire, England, and of Ballykean, County Wicklow, Ireland, together with An Account of Their

Known Descendants in the British Isles and the United States of America to the Year 1961. 1961. Reviewed in NYR 93-2, p 122-3; TAG 38-2, p 115

McGee, Charles M., Jr., and Ernest M. Lander. A Rebel Came Home. 1961. Rev Reviewed in SCH 63-4, p 240-1

McGee, Dorothy Horton. Raynham Hall (1738-1960): Oyster Bay, L. I. 1961. Reviewed in NYR 93-1, p 58-9

Maissin, Eugene. The French in Mexico and Texas, 1838-1839. Reviewed in STI 2-3, p 111-12

Marsh, Kenneth Frederick, and Blanche Marsh. Historic Flat Rock: Where the Old South Lingers. 1961. Reviewed in 63-2, p 117-8

Mecklenburg Co., Va., Marriage Records, 1811-1853. 1962. Prestwould Chapter, DAR. Reviewed in VG 6-4, p 181; VGA 12 Oct. 1962

Mayflower Descendant, Index of Persons, Vols. 1-34, of the. Vol. I, A -G (1959); Vol. II, H - Z (1962). Reviewed in NYR 93-3, p 188

Meyer, Duane. The Highland Scots of North Carolina, 1732-1776. 1961. R Reviewed in NCR 39-2, p 222; SCH 63-3, p 186-7; VA 70-3, p 358; WM 19-3, p 483-4

Meyer, Mrs. Harold I. Roster of Revolutionary War Soldiers and Widows Who Lived in Illinois Counties. 1962. Reviewed in VG 6-4, p 182.

Mote, Luke Smith. Early Settlement of Friends in the Miami Valley. 1961. Reviewed in TAG 38-1, p 62

Mowrer, Lillian T. The Indomitable John Scott: Citizen of Long Island, 1632-1704. 1960. Reviewed in NYR 93-2, p 118-19

Mudgett, Mildred D., and Bruce D. Mudgett. Thomas Mudgett of Salisbury, Mass., and His Descendants. 1961. Reviewed in TAG 38-4, p 250; VG 6-1, p 42-3

Munn, Robert F. Index to West Virginiana, 1960. Reviewed in MHM 57-1, p 65

Munn, Robert F. The Southern Appalachians: A Bibliography & Guide to Studies. 1961. Reviewed in NCR 39-3, p 399-400

Murtaugh, Paul. Your Irish Coat-of-Arms. 1960. Reviewed in NYR 93-3, p 187

National Society DAR. Is That Lineage Right? 1958. Reviewed in NM 1-1, p 15

Neel, Eurie Pearl Wilford. The Statistical Handbook of Trigg Co., Ky., The Gateway to the Jackson Purchase in Kentucky and Tennessee. 1961. Reviewed in ANS 9-1, p 9; FC 36-2, p 188; KG 4-2, p 76; RK 60-3, p 237-8

Nelson, Martha Eunice Ensign. Record of the Descendants of James Ensign and His Wife, Sarah Elson, 1634-1939-1960. 1960. Reviewed in STI 2-1, p 36

Nelson, Walter R. History of Goshen, N. H. 1957. Reviewed in NYR 93-2, p 120-21

New Orleans, Genealogical Research Society of. New Orleans Genesis. Jan., 1962. Reviewed in NGS 50-3, p 166

Oklahoma Genealogical Society Quarterly. July issue reviewed in VGA 19 Oct. September issue reviewed in VGA 28 Dec.

Oregon Donation Land Claims, Genealogical Material in. Vol. III. Reviewed in SEA 12-2, p 200

Orvin, Maxwell Clayton. In South Carolina Waters, 1861-1865. 1961. Reviewed in SCH 63-2, p 117

Parker, John. Van Meteren's Virginia, 1607-1612. 1961. Reviewed in NCR 39-2, p 229

Patton, Sadie Smathers. A Condensed History of Flat Rock. 1961. Reviewed in NCR 39-2, p 225

Peale Museum, The. Baltimore During the Civil War. 1961. Reviewed in MDG 3-4, p 85

Percy, Alfred. The Amherst County Story: A Virginia Saga. 1961. Reviewed in VA 70-1, p 107

Peterson, Clarence Stewart. Consolidated Bibliography of County Histories in Fifty States in 1961. Reviewed in NYR 93-2, p 124.

Pine, L. G. American Origins. 1960. Reviewed in NGS 50-3, p 163-4; NYR 93-1, p 60.

Place, Frank. Index of Personal Names in J. H. French's Gazetteer of the State of N. Y. (1860) 1962. Reviewed in SEA 12-2, p 200; STI 2-4, p 132

Pollock, Polly. Asters at Dusk: The Smelser Family in America. 1961. Reviewed in NYR 93-2, p 124

Prindle, Paul W. An Account of A Search for the Identity of Mary Morey, Wife of Timothy Crosby. (Supplement to Bulletin of the Stamford, Conn. Genealogical Society) Reviewed in TAG 38-2, p 115

Pumfret, John E. The Province of East New Jersey, 1609-1702: The Rebellious Proprietary. 1962. Reviewed in TAG 38-4, p 252-3

Reed, C. Wingate. Beaufort County: Two Centuries of Its History. 1962. Reviewed in NCR 39-4, p 556-7

Report: Ohio Genealogical Society. Reviewed in VGA 30 Nov.

Reynolds, J. A. Heraldry and You: Modern Heraldic Usage in America. 1961. Reviewed in NE Oct., p 289-90; NGS 50-3, p 158-62

Richards, John A. A History of Bath Co., Ky. 1961. Reviewed in FC 36-1, p 56; RK 60-3, p 238-41

Roglance, Ward J. Remingtons of Utah, with their Ancestors and Descendants. 1960. Reviewed in NYR 93-3, p 185

Rohrbough, Fred Ware. The Rohrbough Family. 1962. Reviewed in LA 9-4, p 54; SGX 3-24, p 4

Rowse, A. L. Sir Walter Ralegh: His Family and Private Life. 1962. Reviewed in STI 2-3, p 110

Royalist Magazine, The. Vol. 1, No. 3, May-June, 1961, Bi-monthly. Reviewed in TAG 38-1, p 62-3

Rubincam, Milton (ed.). Genealogical Research: Methods and Sources. 1960. Reviewed in LA 9-2, p 26; NGS 50-1, p 46

Rutland, Robert Allen. George Mason: Reluctant Statesman. 1961. Reviewed in NYR 93-3, p 186-7

Salem County Historical Society Publications, Vol. 2, No. 1. Old Deeds Belonging to the Salem County Historical Society. 1961. Reviewed in TAG 38-3, p 191

Sanders, Mary Elizabeth. Records of Attakapas District, La., 1739-1811. 1962. Reviewed in LA 9-2, p 26

Sanders, Robert Stuart. Robert Stuart and His Descendants. 1962. Reviewed in FC 36-4, p 356

Saunders, Robert Stuart. Presbyterianism in Paris and Bourbon Co., Ky., 1786-1961. 1961. Reviewed in FC 36-1, p 57

Scott, W. W. A History of Orange Co., Va. 1962. Reviewed in VG 6-4, p 181

Seversmith, Herbert F., and Kenn Stryker-Rodda. Long Island Genealogical Source Material (A Bibliography). Special Publication of NGS. 1962. Reviewed in DS 26-2, p 86; LIH 2-2, p 59-60; NE Oct., p 292-3; NGS 50-2, p 111; TAG 38-4, p 249-50; VG 6-3, p 137-8

Sevier, Cora Bales, and Nancy Sevier Madden. Sevier Family History with the Letters of Gen. John Sevier, First Governor of Tennessee and 28 Collateral Family Lineages. Reviewed in MDG 3-2, p 48

Sharpe, Bill. A New Geography of North Carolina. Vol. III. 1961. Reviewed in NCR 39-2, p 223-4

Sheldon, Carew. The Sheldon Magazine. (reprinted with corrections & additions) 1957. Reviewed in TAG 38-4, p 251

Sherman, Nell Watson. The Maupin Family, with Allied Branches. 1962. Reviewed in FC 36-3, p 286

Shetler, Charles. Guide to the Study of West Virginia History. 1960. Reviewed in MHM 57-1, p 65

Shipton, Clifford K. Biographical Sketches of Those Who Attended Harvard College in the Classes 1741-1745, with Biographical and Other Notes. 1960 Reviewed in WM 19-3, p 453-4

Smallwood, Graham T. Hereditary Order of the Descendants of Colonial Governors. 1962. Reviewed in NYR 93-3, p 186

Smith, Warren B. White Servitude in South Carolina. 1961. Reviewed in SCH 63-1, p 116

Stancliff, Mary Harrel. Marriage Bonds of Nelson Co., Ky., 1785-1832. Vol. 1 (A - J). 1962. Reviewed in FC 36-2, p 190; KG 4-2, p 76-7; VG 6-3, p 137

Steenrod, Robert L. Boone County, Ill., Marriage Records, 1838-1860. 1960. Reviewed in NGS 50-1, p 45

Stein, Simon Gerberich. The Steins of Muscatine (Iowa). 1961. Reviewed in DS 26-2, p 86; PGM 22-4, p 281-2

Sweeny, Lenora Higginbotham. Marriage Records of Amherst Co., Va., 1815-1821, and Subscription for Building St. Mark's Church, Amherst Co., Va. 1961. Reviewed in VG 6-2, p 86

Syrett, Harold C. (ed.). The Papers of Alexander Hamilton, Vol. I: 1768-1788. 1961. Reviewed in STI 2-1, p 36-7

Talbert, Charles Gano. Benjamin Logan: Kentucky Frontiersman. 1962. Reviewed in FC 36-4, p 355-6; RK 60-4, p 321-2; NCR 39-4, p 561-2

Taylor, Donald Ransone. Out of the Past - The Future: A History of Hampton, Va. 1960. Reviewed in VA 70-1, p 106

Temple, Sarah B. Gober, and Kenneth Coleman. Georgia Journeys. 1961. Reviewed in TAG 38-3, p 191.

Terrill, Helen Eliza, and Dixon, Sara Robertson. History of Stewart Co., Ga. (Section I by Helen Eliza Terrill, Section II by Sara Robertson Dixon) 1958 Reviewed in VG 6-3, p 139

Texas State Genealogical Society. Stirpes. March 1961 issue reviewed in NGS 50-3, p 166; March 1962 issue reviewed in VGA 7 Sept. 1962

Thompson, Katherine Wilcox. Penfield's Past, 1810-1960. 1960. Reviewed in NYR 93-1, p 59-60

Toll-Wolcott Ancestors in America. 1961. Reviewed in TAG 38-1, p 62

Townsend, Mrs. Charles D., and Donald Lines Jacobus. "Current Genealogical Periodicals" in American Genealogist, Vol. 38, p 116-28. Reviewed in DS 25-4, p 176; VG 6-3, p 136

Turabian, Kate L. A Manual for Writers of Term Papers, Theses, and Dissertations. 1961. Reviewed in STI 2-2, p 67

Turnbull, Andrew. Scott Fitzgerald. 1962. Reviewed in STI 2-4, p 132

Unett, John. Making a Pedigree. 1961. Reviewed in STI 2-4, p 132-3

Vann, Elizabeth Chapman Denny, and Margaret Collins Denny Dixon. Brumback-Hotsinpiller Genealogy. 1961. Reviewed in NGS 50-1, p 43; VG 6-1, p 41-2

Vann, Elizabeth Chapman Denny, and Margaret Collins Denny Dixon. Virginia's First German Colony. 1961. Reviewed in STI 2-2, p 67

Van Tassel, David D. Recording America's Past: An Interpretation of the Development of Historical Studies in America, 1607-1884. 1960. Reviewed in MHM 57-2, p 169-70

Vidrine, Jacqueline Olivier, and Winston De Ville. Marriage Contracts of the Opelousas Post, 1766-1803. 1960. Reviewed in LA 9-2, p 19-20

Wagner, Sir Anthony Richard. English Ancestry. 1961. Reviewed in NE April, p 148; NGS 50-2, p 111-13; TAG 38-1, p 59-61; TAG 38-2, p 114; VA 70-2, p 199

Walker, Emma Jane, and Virginia Wilson. Kentucky Bible Records, Vol. One: From the Files of the Genealogical Records Committee, Kentucky Society, DAR. 1962. Reviewed in FC 36-3, p 292; RK 60-3, p 245-6; KG 4-3, p 117; VG 6-3, p 139; VGA July 13, 1962

Warner, Pauline Pearce. Benjamin Harrison of Berkeley, Walter Cocke of Surry, Family Records I. 1962. Reviewed in VG 6-2, p 83-4

Washington, George. Strickland and Neville (reprinted from Cumberland and Westmorland Antiquarian and Archaeological Society's Transactions, vol. LXI, New Series) Reviewed in TAG 38-3, p 192

Wertenbaker, Thomas J. Norfolk: Historic Southern Port. 1962. VA 70-4, p 489-92

White, Kathrine Keogh. King's Mountain Men. 1924. Reviewed in NM 1-1, p 15

Williams, Ethel W. Know Your Ancestors: A Guide to Genealogical Research. Reviewed in STI 2-3, p 112-13

Williams, George W. Early Ministers at St. Michael's, Charleston. 1961. Reviewed in SCH 63-1, p 57-8

Wingo, Elizabeth B. Collection of Unrecorded Wills, Norfolk Co., Va., 1711-1800. Reviewed in VG 6-1, p 41

Wingo, Elizabeth B. Marriages of Norfolk Co., Va., 1706-1792, Vol. 1. 1961. Reviewed in VG 6-1, p 41

Wingo, Elizabeth B. Marriages of Princess Anne Co., Va., 1749-1821. 1961. Reviewed in VG 6-2, p 87

Wulfeck, Dorothy Ford. Carter of Virginia. 1962. Reviewed in VGA 7 Dec.

Wulfeck, Dorothy Ford. *Hawkins of Virginia, North Carolina and Kentucky.* 1962. Reviewed in VGA 25 May 1962

Wulfeck, Dorothy Ford. *Marriages of Some Virginia Residents, 1607-1800: Series I, Vol. 1 (A to B).* 1962. Reviewed in VGA 9 Nov. 1962

Yesteryears: A Quarterly Magazine for the Appreciation and Study of New York Regional History. Vol. 5, No. 18, Dec. 1961, reviewed in TAG *38-3*, p 192; Vol. 5, Nos. 18 and 19, Dec. 1961 and March 1962, reviewed in TAG *38-4*, p 251

Addenda

Ball, Bonnie Sage. *Red Trails and White.* 1955. Reviewed in VGA 17 Aug. 1962

Louisville, University of. *Old Louisville (Ky.).* 1961. Reviewed in KG *4-1*, p 37-8